Programmed Learning Aid for

BASIC
PROGRAMMING
LANGUAGE

Programmed Learning Aid for

BASIC PROGRAMMING LANGUAGE

Revised Edition

ALLEN H. BRADY
Professor of Mathematics
University of Nevada, Reno

JAMES T. RICHARDSON
Professor of Sociology
University of Nevada, Reno

Coordinating Editor
ROGER H. HERMANSON
Georgia State University

LEARNING SYSTEMS COMPANY

A division of
RICHARD D. IRWIN, INC.   Homewood, Illinois   60430

Also available through

IRWIN-DORSEY LIMITED   Georgetown, Ontario   L7G 4B3

ISBN 0-256-02124-4

Printed in the United States of America

1 2 3 4 5 6 7 8 9 0 K 8 7 6 5 4 3 2 1

FOREWORD

Learning a programming language such as BASIC is often necessary. This PLAID was created to provide you with an effective, efficient, and interesting means of accomplishing this task.

This PLAID, as do all other PLAIDs in this series, applies the powerful tool of programmed learning to the subject matter. The method of programming is easy to use and has the following advantages:

1. Correct responses to concepts are *reinforced immediately*.
2. Incorrect interpretations of concepts are *corrected immediately*.
3. The reader is kept *active* in the studying process and this increases his interest level and comprehension.
4. The method makes studying seem like a game.

This PLAID on BASIC was used in test form by a large number of students who praised its effectiveness.

PLAIDs are continuously updated in new printings to provide the reader with the latest subject matter content in the field.

Professor Allen Brady teaches computer science courses for the Department of Mathematics, University of Nevada, Reno. He was formerly assistant director of the university computer center and was instrumental in the introduction of the BASIC language to the educational users on various university campuses and high schools which used those facilities starting in 1968. He has been professionally involved with computers since 1961 and involved with microcomputer applications for five years. Professor James Richardson has been teaching in the area of computer applications and statistics at the University of Nevada, Reno since 1968 and has also served as chairman of the Department of Sociology there.

ROGER H. HERMANSON
Coordinating Editor and Programmer

PREFACE

This book focuses on the BASIC programming language which is found on most time-sharing computers and personal microcomputers. The BASIC language (Beginners All-Purpose Symbolic Instruction Code) was developed at Dartmouth College under a project sponsored by the National Science Foundation and directed by John G. Kemeny and Thomas E. Kurtz. BASIC has proved itself a boon to educational computing throughout the country because of the ease with which it is learned and the wide number of tasks to which it can be applied. From the time of its beginning with the introduction of computer time-sharing to the present day personal computer revolution, BASIC has attained prominence as the most widely learned, taught, and used programming language in existence.

Computer time-sharing enables one computer to serve many different users simultaneously. These users are typically located at remote typewriter terminals attached by telephone lines or other means to the main computer. In time-sharing, the computer gives each person the impression that he is the exclusive user of his own machine. With the advent of personal microcomputers, such an exclusive situation has become a reality. It was only natural that the BASIC language, with its attendant simple commands, should become the first and main language of these microcomputers. Along with the original appendix on time-sharing use, we have added an appendix in this edition which gives step by step details for running BASIC programs on the three currently most popular microcomputer systems found in schools and homes.

This text was developed from a precursor which had several years of testing in the classroom at the University of Nevada, Reno. The introductory section of our early classroom notes followed, in part, a brief set of instructional notes written by John Nevison and distributed by Dartmouth College in 1968. As our classroom notes were greatly expanded and rewritten, they nevertheless retained the general initial approach of the Dartmouth notes. The influence upon the style of the first few chapters of this book is therefore gratefully acknowledged.

While directed primarily toward nontechnical undergraduate students in universities, our book has been successfully used in high schools and has demonstrated its value as a self-instructional text for graduate students and for faculty, including scientific researchers. It has also been used successfully in community college and extension courses and by laymen and businessmen who want to know something about computing. At the university level the text has been used in sociology, psychology, business, agriculture, mathematics, education, and other areas.

Typically, the use of these materials has been as an accompanying supplement to a substantive course such as statistics. This has worked out well in most instances because of the self-instructional nature of the presentation. Our earlier experience in the classroom plus six years of successful use of the first PLAID edition had demonstrated that the self-instructional approach we use is functional and that many people have been able to learn the fundamentals of computing with the BASIC language using this approach along with the programmed learning technique that is featured in the PLAID series.

The main body of the book includes 14 chapters that increase in difficulty as one proceeds through the text. We recommend that the student start at the beginning and work his way through (instead of jumping around), because we have presented the language in a cumulative way, following the chapter sequence. Some students will find that the last two chapters will not be of use to them because they incorporate some of the more advanced features of the language. There are other features of the BASIC language that are not incorporated in our book, but many of these are somewhat system-specific and represent things that would be very difficult to describe in a general sort of way.

In each of the 14 chapters the student will find two helpful learning devices. First, a number of programming and other problems are included in the chapters. When these are to be done on the computer, they should be carried out before proceeding further·in the text. Then there are a number of fill-in-the-blank questions in each chapter, with answers to the questions in the margins. This programmed learning approach will help students learn the materials presented in the associated frame.

Appendix A gives general instructions for the use of time-sharing terminals. It also discusses paper tape equipment found on the many teletypewriter terminals still in use. This appendix (or Appendix D if working with a microcomputer) should be studied as soon as the student is ready to begin with the programming exercises. Appendix B contains a number of case studies which will have appeal to students from different disciplines. These case studies are cross-referenced with the materials in the 14 chapters so that the student can find illustrations of things that have been learned in these chapters. We recommend that after finishing the text, the student examine each of the case studies and run the programs. Appendix C is a comparison of several BASIC versions to aid the student in working with a specific implementation of the language.

Appendix D gives instructions for running BASIC programs on the Apple computer using Applesoft II (trademark of Apple Computers, Inc.), the CBM PET computer (CBM and PET are trademarks of Commodore Business Machines, Inc.), and the Radio Shack TRS-80 microcomputer using LEVEL II BASIC (TRS-80 is a trademark of Tandy Corporation).

The Glossary/Index is a summary of major features of the BASIC language. This useful guide gives all of the instructions in the BASIC language that have been presented and cross-references them with the text. Therefore it serves not only as a summary but also as an index for the book.

We express our appreciation to the many students and teachers who, over the last several years, have used various versions of the text and supplied us with useful comments and occasional corrections. We are grateful to the many instructors who had confidence in the earlier edition of the material and chose to use it in their classes. Finally, we thank Apple, Commodore, and Tandy Corporation for giving us permission to quote from their reference manuals (see Appendix D) in preparing the instructions on using microcomputers, and we express our gratitude to the Byte Shop of Reno and the Park Lane Radio Shack for providing access to the microcomputers described in the appendix.

A. H. BRADY
J. T. RICHARDSON

TOPICAL OUTLINE OF COURSE CONTENT

CONTENTS

Introduction

1 _____

BASIC is a simple language used for giving instructions to a computer. An individual BASIC instruction is called a *statement*. A set of instructions or statements one gives to a computer is called a *program*. The process of determining what statements to give a computer to carry out a desired calculation is called *programming*.

In this text you will be introduced to the various types of BASIC statements and have the opportunity to use them in programs of your own. By following the examples, you will learn something of the thinking that takes place in the process of programming. Before proceeding, however, you may find it helpful to obtain a BASIC reference manual for your specific computer.

There are several different kinds of BASIC statements. In the course of this text all of them will be explained, beginning with those that are the most useful in getting you started using a computer.

An individual BASIC instruction is called a _____.   statement

A set of statements is a _____.   program

A simple program

1 _____

Let us examine a simple BASIC program for computing the average of the numbers 12, 5, and 10:

```
5   PRINT "FIRST PROGRAM BY JOHN SMITH"
10  LET A = (12+5+10)/3
15  PRINT A
20  END
```

The statements are *executed* (carried out) in order from top to bottom. First the legend in statement 5 is printed. Then statement number 10 performs the desired calculation, letting quantity A equal the result. In statement 15 the value which was assigned to A is printed. Statement 20 is an END statement. It must be the very last statement in a BASIC program.

All statements in a BASIC program must be numbered with unique numbers which may range from 1 to 9999. The statements are arranged in the order of their numbers from the lowest at the beginning to the highest at the END.

Every program statement must have a _____.

The statement numbers must be _____.

The statements are arranged in the order of their _____.

> number
>
> unique
>
> numbers (from lowest to highest)

PROBLEM 1.1 _____

Your first assignment is to run the above program on your computer and obtain the answer. If you have a computer time-sharing terminal, follow the instructions on using time-sharing given in Appendix A. Otherwise, follow the instructions for your microcomputer system given in Appendix D.

Before you proceed, note that blanks or spaces in BASIC statements are ignored by the computer. The programmer may intersperse blank spaces where he feels they will help make the program more readable. However, blanks within text in quotes (as in the PRINT statement 5 above) are *not* ignored, and remain part of the text.

In BASIC programs the computer ignores _____, except when they appear within _____.

In a PRINT statement, everything within quotation marks is _____.

> blanks
> quotation marks
>
> printed exactly as written

The READ and DATA statements

1 _____

The program given in Chapter 1 could have been written as follows:

```
 6  READ B
 7  READ C, D
10  LET A = (B+C+D)/3
15  PRINT A
16  DATA 12, 5
18  DATA 10
20  END
```

This program does the same computation as the one in the previous section. However, it uses the READ and DATA statements. Statements 6 and 7 are READ statements. If READ statements are used, there must be one or more DATA statements in the program, as seen here in statements 16 and 18.

The computer responds to a READ statement by giving values to the variables listed. The values assigned are taken in order from the lists of values supplied in the DATA statements. Note that values in a DATA statement are separated by commas.

In the program shown, the computer reads B in statement 6 and assigns to B the value 12 from DATA statement 16. Next, the computer reads C and D in statement 7, assigns to C the value 5 from DATA statement 16, and assigns to D the value 10 from DATA statement 18.

If READ statements are used in a program, then there must also be one or more
_____ statements.

DATA

2 _____

Note that statements 6 and 7 could have been combined into one READ statement. Likewise, statements 16 and 18 could have been combined into a single DATA statement.

```
 6  READ B,C,D
10  LET A = (B+C+D)/3
15  PRINT A
16  DATA 12, 5, 10
20  END
```

The rule to remember is that the DATA numbers are assigned to the variables in the exact order that the variables are READ by the computer in *executing* (running) the program. The numbers in all of the DATA statements are simply treated together as one long list of numbers. From this list, numbers are extracted in sequence as needed by the READ statements.

If the program above had contained the statement 16 DATA 11, 17, 2, then B would have been given the value ⎯⎯⎯, C the value ⎯⎯⎯, and D the value ⎯⎯⎯.

11   17
2

PROBLEM 2.1 _____

Run the preceding program using your own set of data. Check your results by hand. In this and all subsequent programs include a PRINT statement that will cause your name and the problem number to print out with the answers.

3 _____

In the preceding examples of programs, the letters A, B, C, and D were used as variable names. Single letters or single letters followed by one digit (0 to 9) may be used to denote variables. Examples of two-character names are W3, X5, and J9. A total of 286 distinct variable names is thus allowed for any one program.

Which of this list are correct variable names?
A12, AB, 3C, C2, X1, XA, B8, 1X1, X12, 22, K

C2, X1, B8, K

Arithmetic operations in BASIC

1 _____

In BASIC, symbols are used to denote the operations of

$+$ addition
$-$ subtraction
$*$ multiplication
$/$ division

In the statement

$$10 \ \text{LET} \ A = B+C-D*E/F$$

all four operations are used. Note that the symbol for multiplication is always explicitly used. You would never write D2 for D*2, since this would be confused with a variable name.

X*Y

If X is to be multiplied by Y, this should be written _____ .

2 _____

In performing BASIC arithmetic operations, the computer follows the usual rules. It first performs any operations enclosed in parentheses. Then it always multiplies and divides before it adds and subtracts. Otherwise, it performs operations from left to right. Applying these rules, you can see that

$$7 - 3 + 6 = 10, \text{ while } 7 - (3 + 6) = -2;$$
$$3 + 2 * 8 = 19, \text{ while } (3 + 2) * 8 = 40;$$
$$5 * 6 / 3 * 2 = 20, \text{ while } 5 * 6 / (3 * 2) = 5.$$

Note: Whenever there is doubt about application of the rules, it is wise to use parentheses to make explicit to the programmer and the computer what is intended.

What are the values of the following, if A = 10, B = 2, C = 7, and D = 3?

9.9
1.5
9.9
8.5

$A + B - C * D/A =$ _____ .
$(A + B - C) * D/A =$ _____ .
$A + B - C * (D/A) =$ _____ .
$A + (B - C) * D/A =$ _____ .

PROBLEM 3.1 _____

Write a program to compute first the product and then the quotient of two numbers and print the results. Use the READ and DATA statements, and make some of the variable names two characters in length.

PROBLEM 3.2 _____

If, in the LET statement (statement 10) of the example in Section 1, the variables B, C, D, E, and F are assigned the values 20, 8, 3, 4, and 5, respectively, what will be the value of A? _____

    Verify your answer by means of a program.

25.6

The GO TO . . . statement

1 _____

The program you wrote for Problem 3.1 could have looked something like this:

```
 5  READ B, C
10  LET A1 = B*C
20  PRINT "PRODUCT IS", A1
30  LET A2 = B/C
40  PRINT "QUOTIENT IS", A2
50  DATA 25, 7
60  END
```

As this program now stands, every time we want to do a computation with a new pair of numbers, we must rerun the program with a new DATA statement. It would be convenient if we could get the computer to repeat the calculation for additional numbers without our intervention. By inserting the line

45 GO TO 5

we can cause the machine to go back to line 5 when it reaches line 45 and begin the program sequence again with 5 READ B, C.

Then, if the DATA statement is changed to

50 DATA 25, 7, 36, 9

the machine will, on the second time through, read the values of 36 and 9 for B and C, respectively, and print a second set of answers. The machine will continue to *loop* back through the program until the list of numbers given in the DATA statement is exhausted. When this occurs, BASIC prints a message like OUT OF DATA, and the program terminates.

With the program modified in the manner suggested, the next statement to be executed after statement 45 will be statement _____.

If the list of numbers given in the DATA statements is exhausted, execution of a READ statement will result in _____.

5

program termination

PROBLEM 4.1 _____

Revise the above program using a GO TO . . . statement, computing in sequence the products and quotients of the following pairs:

```
14, 7
35, 3
−4, 5
14, −5
```

The IF . . . THEN . . . statement

1 _____

In Problem 4.1, it may have occurred to you that there was a possibility of having a pair of data numbers which would result in a division by zero.

Note that computers are not consistent on the matter of division by zero. This varies from one machine to another and from one programming language to another. Sometimes the machine is made to halt, sometimes it is made to print out a message, and sometimes it will yield an unpredictable result and continue running. Thus division by zero should be the programmer's concern.

IF division by zero were going to occur, THEN you should do something special about it. In BASIC, the IF . . . THEN . . . statement provides for the detection of this and various other specifiable situations (conditions). It will cause the computer to *jump* out of the normal program sequence if the condition occurs.

The IF . . . THEN . . . statement has the form

IF *condition* THEN *statement number*

The statement number to the right of THEN will be the statement to which the computer goes IF the condition specified is true. Thus, the statement

25 IF C = 0 THEN 60

inserted in the program of Chapter 4 will result in the program's halting after it prints.

PRODUCT IS 0

whenever the value read for C is zero. That is, if C is zero when statement 25 is executed, the next statement executed will be

60 END

and the computer will stop your program. If, however, it is not true that C is zero, then the next statement in sequence following 25 will be executed. In this case, that would be

30 LET A2 = B/C

and the program will continue as before.

The _____ statement allows a check for important conditions in a program (such as division by zero).

2

An alternative to the statement 25 we just devised would be the following:

$$25 \ \text{IF} \ C = 0 \ \text{THEN} \ 5$$

The effect of this statement 25 would be to cause the computer to jump to the beginning of the program in the event C is zero, avoiding the division by zero but continuing the running of the program. (See Problem 5.2 below.)

PROBLEM 5.1

Add the statement

$$25 \ \text{IF} \ C = 0 \ \text{THEN} \ 60$$

to your program of Problem 4.1, and run the program with the following set of data:

$$14, 2, -3, 6, 4, 0, 21, 3, 13, 2$$

PROBLEM 5.2

Replace the statement 25 with

$$25 \ \text{IF} \ C = 0 \ \text{THEN} \ 5$$

in the program of Problem 5.1, and run it with the same data. What is the difference between the programs? _____

_____

_____

The first program (Problem 5.1) halts when the zero division is encountered. The second program (Problem 5.2) skips the division by zero and continues running.

3

There are conditions other than *equals* which may be used in an IF . . . THEN . . . statement. The complete list of *relations* and their symbols is as follows:

$$=$$ is equal to
$$<$$ is less than
$$>$$ is greater than
$$< =$$ is less than or equal to
$$> =$$ is greater than or equal to
$$<>$$ is not equal to

Examples of conditions which might appear in an IF . . . THEN . . . statement are

$$A<0$$
$$B = C$$
$$B<>C$$
$$3*X = Y+2$$

Write a proper BASIC statement which says in symbolic form, **If** A is greater than or equal to B, then go to statement 90. _____

20 IF A> = B THEN 90

Write a proper BASIC statement which says, in symbolic form, If X is less than Y, then go to statement 30. _____.

60 IF X < Y THEN 30

PROBLEM 5.3 _____

Write a program using IF . . . THEN . . . statements and appropriate relational operators which reads and compares pairs of numbers, printing THE FIRST NUMBER IS GREATER THAN THE SECOND, or THE TWO NUMBERS ARE EQUAL, or THE SECOND NUMBER IS GREATER THAN THE FIRST in each case, as appropriate. Test your program on the pairs of numbers below:

$$0, 3$$
$$5, 8$$
$$-6, -2$$
$$4, 4$$
$$-3, 3$$
$$2, 1$$

Hint: This program will require the use of a READ and a DATA statement, IF . . . THEN . . . statements, PRINT statements, and GO TO . . . statements.

chapter
6

Control of program loops

1 —————————————————————

As we have seen in the examples above, it is not necessary to write out every step in a repetitive calculation. We can instruct the computer to *loop* or go back through a series of steps, repeating the process as many times as desired. In the program of Problem 4.1, a process was repeated until all DATA were exhausted by the READ statement. In the program of Problem 5.1, a repeating process was terminated when a specified condition (divisor = zero) was detected by an IF . . . THEN . . . statement.

Loops in a program are frequently used to carry out a number of repeated steps leading to a final result. In the program examples given above, a separate result was computed and printed for each time through the loop. A BASIC program can also compute one result through the use of a repeated loop. An example is computation of the sum of an arbitrarily long list of data numbers.

Assume that the data numbers to be summed have in common some simple characteristic, such as being positive. This will permit the use of a special value, such as zero, to act as a *sentinel,* indicating the end of the sequence of numbers. Its appearance can be detected through use of an IF . . . THEN . . . statement.

```
10  LET  S = 0
20  READ  D
30  IF  D = 0  THEN  60
40  LET  S = S+D
50  GO  TO  20
60  PRINT  "SUM = ",  S
70  DATA  3, 10, 13, 1, 6, 8
80  DATA  0
90  END
```

Examining the program, we see that the variable S will be used to accumulate the sum. S is set equal to zero initially in statement 10. The machine then reads a data item D in statement 20. Statement 30 checks to see if D is equal to zero, which would indicate that the program has reached the sentinel. Since D will have the value 3, the next statement below, statement 40, will be executed. Here D is added to the current total, S, letting S equal the sum. (Since $S = 0$, $S + D = 0 + 3 = 3$. We let S = this value, so now S = 3.)

Then the machine goes back to statement 20 to repeat the process, reading a new D, checking to see whether or not the D is zero, and adding D to S if it is not. The loop will repeat for the data values 10, 13, 1, 6, and 8, going back finally to read a data value D equal to zero. When statement 30 is then executed, the fact that $D = 0$ will cause a jump to statement 60, which will print the final total. The program will stop at statement 90.

If S has the value 3 and D has the value 10 before the execution of

40 LET S = S+D

what will be the value of S afterward? _____

13

After the third time through the loop in the above program, D will have the value _____ and S will have the value_____ .

13   26

PROBLEM 6.1

Run the program above on the computer. Check the result by hand. Run the program above with your own set of data. Check the result by hand.

If the numbers 8, 6, 2, 0, 5, 12 were used in DATA statement 70, would this program give the correct result? _____

No

Why not? _____
_____

Because the program will take the first zero as the sentinel and will stop too soon.

If instead of using zero for a sentinel for this data set we decided to use −1 (minus one), how would we change the program at statement 30? _____
_____

30 IF D = −1 THEN 60

How would we change statement 80? _____

80 DATA −1

2

With a simple modification of the preceding program, we can obtain a count of the number of data items. If we let the variable C stand for the count and initially set C = 0, we can add 1 to C each time through the loop. We add the statements

15 LET C = 0
45 LET C = C+1

to the program along with a new print statement:

60 PRINT "SUM OF", C, "NUMBERS = ", S

PROBLEM 6.2

Make the above changes to the program used in Problem 6.1 and run it on the computer. Run it also with your own data set.

PROBLEM 6.3

With the final values of S and C, we can compute the average of the numbers in the data list. Modify the program of Problem 6.2 by adding one or more statements to compute and print the average of the C numbers. Run this program on the computer with both the given data set and your own.

Following
statement 60

Where would the statements to compute and print the average be placed? _____
_____

3 _____

It is not always easy to handle input data with a sentinel. For the programs described above it was arbitrarily assumed that no values of zero would appear in the data. Thus it was easy to use zero as a sentinel. If zero could appear in the data (along with negative numbers), however, the sentinel would have to be some large number known to be outside the range of the data. If the range is not known or can vary, then it may be necessary to read in as data the number of remaining data items to be handled.

The following program does exactly that. It reads N first, where N stands for the number of data items (6). It controls the loop by checking the count, C, against the number of items, N, to be read.

```
10 LET  S = 0
15 LET  C = 0
20 READ N
30 IF  C = N  THEN  60
35 READ D
40 LET  S = S+D
45 LET  C = C+1
50 GO TO 30
60 PRINT "SUM = "; S; "AVERAGE = "; S/N
70 DATA 6
80 DATA 3, 10, 13, 1, 6, 8
90 END
```

Note the use of the expression, S/N, in the PRINT statement, 60. This is another feature of the PRINT statement. We also separated the items by means of semicolons instead of commas. This will result in a more closely spaced printout.

outside the range
of the data

If a particular number value is to serve as a sentinel to indicate the end of a data list, then the value chosen for the sentinel must be _____
_____.

PROBLEM 6.4 _____

Run the above program as shown. Also run it to obtain the sum and average of the numbers 3, 6, 2, 0, 8, 12, 4.

70 DATA 7

How would we change 70 for this new list? _____

4 _____

Data are not always required in a program. It is sometimes possible to generate the necessary data using a loop. In the following program a table of square roots is printed for the numbers from 1 to 10. These numbers are generated by counting as the program goes through the loop.

```
5  REM-TABLE OF SQUARES AND SQUARE ROOTS
10 LET X = 0
20 LET X = X+1
30 PRINT X, X↑2, SQR(X)
40 IF X<10 THEN 20
50 END
```

The program continues back through the loop until X reaches the value of 10. Each time through, the computer will print the value of X, X-squared (X to the 2nd power is written X↑2), and the square root of X, obtained by writing SQR(X).

Note that the symbol ↑ does appear on time-sharing terminals but it does not appear on key punches. Some versions of BASIC will allow two asterisks ** to be used in place of ↑. (See Appendix C.)

PROBLEM 6.5 _____

Run the program above. Then modify it to yield a table for the numbers up to and including 25.

5 _____

The REM statement (which stands for remark) used in the preceding program is *not* executed by the computer. It provides a way to insert explanations or remarks in the *listing* of a program to aid in interpretation. The REM must not be confused with statements such as

220 PRINT "FINAL SUM"

which are executable and which serve the function of making the *output* of a program interpretable.

A statement such as

20 REM-TABLE OF SUMS

is for the benefit of someone trying to understand the _____.   program listing
This statement (does, does not) cause anything to be printed on the sheet of   does not
output.

A statement such as

20 PRINT "TABLE OF SUMS"

is to help make the _____ readable and understand-   output or results
able.

The FOR and NEXT statements

1 _____

Because loops controlled by counting occur so frequently in programs, special statements have been defined in BASIC for creating and controlling such loops. These are the FOR and NEXT statements. The program example in Text Frame 4 of Chapter 6 could more easily have been written as follows:

```
5   REM-TABLE OF SQUARES AND SQUARE ROOTS
15  FOR X = 1 TO 10
20  PRINT X, X↑2, SQR(X)
30  NEXT X
40  END
```

The FOR statement above calls for the execution of all statements which follow down to the NEXT statement, first for $X = 1$, then for $X = 2$, then for $X = 3$, etc., and finally for $X = 10$. The NEXT X statement brackets the statements which are to be repeatedly executed for each value of X. There must always be a NEXT statement to correspond to a FOR statement.

Had we desired the table for only even numbers, we could have written:

```
15  FOR X = 2 TO 10 STEP 2
```

for statement 15. In this case the calculation would begin with $X = 2$ and then repeat for $X = 4$, $X = 6$, $X = 8$ and finally $X = 10$. When no STEP is specified, a value of +1 is assumed for the step.

Negative steps are permitted. Thus, we might have produced the table in inverse order by using the statement

```
15  FOR X = 10 TO 1 STEP −1
```

The statement

```
15  FOR X = 1 TO 5
```

would cause the statements between it and the NEXT X statement to execute _____ times.

The statement

```
15  FOR C = 3 TO 12 STEP 3
```

would cause the statements between it and the corresponding NEXT C statement to execute _____ times.

5

4

PROBLEM 7.1 _____

Run the new squares and square roots program in this chapter using the various versions of the FOR statement that were shown.

2 _____

Variables are also permitted as the starting and ending values and for the step. Thus, we can generalize our squares and square roots program as follows:

```
 5  REM-TABLE OF SQUARES AND SQUARE ROOTS
10  READ A, B, C
15  FOR X = A TO B STEP C
20  PRINT X, X↑2, SQR(X)
30  NEXT X
35  DATA 1, 25, 2
40  END
```

Step values and starting and ending values in the FOR statement may all be _____.

In the program above the value for C is _____.

variables

2

PROBLEM 7.2 _____

Run the program above as shown and also with data of 36, 0, −3.

3 _____

You may be considering the possibility of *nesting* FOR statements, that is, placing one loop inside another. This is permitted so long as the loops are nested properly: they may not partially overlap or cross. You can *never* include just a FOR statement inside a larger outside loop. The FOR statement must be accompanied by its own NEXT statement within the larger loop. A *correct* example is given below.

```
10  FOR X = 1 TO 4
20  PRINT X
30  FOR Y = 1 TO 3
40  PRINT X, Y
50  NEXT Y
60  NEXT X
```

Each FOR in a program must have a corresponding _____ statement.

Nested loops may not _____.

NEXT

partially overlap
or cross

PROBLEM 7.3 _____

Include the above example of nested loops in a program, and run it.

Arithmetic expressions in BASIC

1 _____

In Chapter 3 we discussed four arithmetic operations, $+$, $-$, $*$, and $/$. Because arithmetic expressions are constrained to one dimension in BASIC, it has been necessary to introduce a fifth operational symbol for raising a number to a power (exponentiation).

Arithmetic expressions: a^2 $(b + 1)^3$

BASIC expressions: $A \uparrow 2$ $(B + 1) \uparrow 3$

Note: See Text Frame 4 in Chapter 6 for punching $\uparrow$ into a card.

(X↑2+Y↑3)↑4   Write $(x^2 + y^3)^4$ as a BASIC expression. _____

2 _____

It is important to understand the hierarchy or order of evaluation of the arithmetic operations within an expression. Evaluation first occurs within parentheses and then in the following order:

1. $\uparrow$ All exponentiation is computed from left to right: 2↑3↑4 is equivalent to $(2\uparrow3)\uparrow4 = 2^{12}$, not to $2\uparrow(3\uparrow4) = 2^{81}$.

2. $*$ $/$ All multiplications and divisions are computed from left to right: 12/3*4 is equivalent to $(12/3)*4 = 16$, not to $12/(3*4) = 1$.

3. $+$ $-$ Additions and subtractions are computed from left to right.

Translate each of the following arithmetic expressions to BASIC expressions:

a. (A+B)/(C−D)

a. $\dfrac{a + b}{c - d}$ _____

b. (A+B)/C↑3

b. $\dfrac{a + b}{c^3}$ _____

c. D−(A+B)/(4*C)

c. $d - \dfrac{a + b}{4c}$ _____

d. (B↑2−4*A*C)/(2*A)

d. $\dfrac{b^2 - 4ac}{2a}$ _____

e. A↑(1/2)*B↑(1/4)
    or A↑.5*B↑.25

e. $a^{\frac{1}{2}}b^{\frac{1}{4}}$ _____

f. A/(B+C/(D−A))

f. $\dfrac{a}{b + \dfrac{c}{d - a}}$ _____

Compute to three places the value of each of the above expressions for corresponding values of the variables as follows:

a. a = 5, b = −8, c = −3, d = 1.5   _____   .667
b. a = 36, b = −9, c = 3   _____   1.
c. a = 29, b = 11, c = 4, d = 5.5   _____   3.
d. a = 2.5, b = 6, c = 3   _____   1.2
e. a = 8, b = 81   _____   8.48
f. a = 1, b = 2, c = 3, d = 4   _____   .333

PROBLEM 8.1

Verify your results for the preceding question with a BASIC program.

3

Constants may be expressed in a condensed notation when the value of a number is awkwardly expressed in ordinary decimal notation. The customary method of expressing awkwardly large or awkwardly small numbers is to apply a power of 10 as a factor, making a corresponding adjustment in the decimal point. Thus,

.0000352 can be written as $.352 \times 10^{-4}$ or as 3.52×10^{-5}
4510000 can be written as 45.1×10^5 or as 451×10^4

BASIC has a special notation for constants which does not require the exponentiation operation. One merely writes E to the right of a numeric value followed by the whole-number power of 10 (positive or negative). Thus,

.0000352 can be written in BASIC as .352E−4 or as 3.52E−5
4510000 can be written as 4.51E6 or as 451E4 or as 451E+4

Express the following constants in a compact form using BASIC E-notation.

a. .00000041   _____   *a.* 41E−8
                                                     or 4.1E−7

b. 351000×10^4 _____   *b.* 351000E4
                                                       or 3.51E9

c. 5,800,000,000   _____   *c.* 5.8E9
                                                       or 5.8E+9

d. 426.8×10^{-9} _____   *d.* 426.8E−9
                                                       or .4268E−6

Special functions in BASIC

1 _____

In most useful numerical computations, special mathematical functions, such as logarithms, square roots, absolute values, sines, and cosines, frequently occur. Several useful functions are provided in BASIC which can be used simply within any arithmetic expression. Following is a list of such functions.

Arithmetic Functions:

SQR(X)   Calculates the square root of the argument X.
$$SQR(25) = 5$$

LOG(X)   Calculates the natural logarithm of the argument X.
$$LOG(25) = \log_e 25$$

LGT(X)   Calculates the common logarithm of the argument X.
$$LGT(25) = \log_{10} 25$$

EXP(X)   Calculates e raised to the Xth power.
$$EXP(20) = e^{20}$$

ABS(X)   Calculates the absolute value of the argument X.
$$ABS(-17) = 17$$

INT(X)   Calculates the integer part of the argument X.
$$INT(-2.7) = -2.$$

Trigonometric Functions:

SIN(X)   Calculates the sine of X, X expressed in radians.
COS(X)   Calculates the cosine of X, X expressed in radians.
TAN(X)   Calculates the tangent of X, X expressed in radians.
ATN(X)   Calculates the arctangent of X; i.e., the arc in radians whose tangent is X.

What are the values of the expressions below?

SQR(2)   _____

ABS(−3.58)   _____

LGT(40)   _____

INT(25.13)   _____

Arguments for the trigonometric functions SIN, COS, and TAN must be expressed in _____ .

$\sqrt{2}$ or 1.414
3.58
$\log_{10} 40$ or 1.602
25

radians

PROBLEM 9.1 _____

Write a BASIC program to compute the value for each of the ten functions of X given above, with X taking on in order the values 3.6, 1.5, and 13.1, and print the results.

2

Note that not only may functions be used within expressions, but expressions may be used within functions. Thus,

$$x + \sqrt{a^2 - b^2}$$

may be written in BASIC as

X+SQR (A↑2−B↑2)

and

$$4 \sin 2T$$

may be written in BASIC as

4*SIN(2*T)

Translate the following mathematical expressions to BASIC expressions:

$x + \sqrt{y + \sin z}$ _____   X+SQR(Y+SIN (Z))

$\dfrac{a - \sqrt{b + c + d}}{\log_e z}$ _____   (A−SQR(B+C+D))/
                                                      LOG (Z)

3

In the computation hierarchy, function evaluation takes place before any arithmetic operations which are outside the function. Thus,

SQR(4+5)*4

yields the value of 12.

The value for SQR(6+10)*2 is _____.   8

The value for SQR(4+SQR(25)) is _____.   3

Translate the following expressions to valid BASIC expressions:

a.	$3x + y$	_____	a. 3*X+Y
b.	$\sqrt{b^2 - 4ac}$	_____	b. SQR(B↑2−4*A*C)
c.	$3e^{a+b}$	_____	c. 3*EXP(A+B)
d.	$\tan 2T$	_____	d. TAN(2*T)
e.	$\sin^2 a$	_____	e. SIN(A)↑2
f.	$\tan^{-1} y$	_____	f. ATN(Y)

Note: If in question *c* you wrote 3*E↑(A+B) your answer would be correct, provided of course E has been assigned the value 2.71828. Questions *e* and *f* provide examples of inconsistencies in ordinary mathematical notation—$\sin^2 a$ is taken to mean $(\sin a)*(\sin a)$, while $\tan^{-1} y$ stands for arctan (y) instead of

$$\frac{1}{\tan y}$$

PROBLEM 9.2

Evaluate the expressions above in a BASIC program run using the following values:
$y = 1, x = 17, a = 2, b = 3, c = -8, t = .392699.$

Lists and tables

1 _____

Frequently programmers will want to maintain for later use in their programs a list of values they have read and used in some computation. For example, suppose we have a list of test scores for a number of students. Using the techniques described in Chapter 6, we can easily calculate an average score for the test by reading in the values one at a time and cumulating a "partial sum" until all test scores have been included. This does not require that we save each individual value.

However, if we desire to find out how much each student deviates from the mean, then we shall have to maintain a "copy" of the data. After the mean is calculated, we can then go back and subtract each score from the mean to get each individual's deviation score. The following program does this:

```
5    REM-STATEMENTS 10 TO 30 READ SCORES INTO LIST A
10   FOR I = 1 TO 10
20   READ A(I)
30   NEXT I
40   DATA 74,82,93,57,89,75,90,78,80,66
45   REM-STATEMENTS 50 TO 80 CUMULATE SCORES
50   LET S = 0
60   FOR I = 1 TO 10
70   LET S = S+A(I)
80   NEXT I
85   REM-STATEMENT 90 CALCULATES THE MEAN SCORE
90   LET S1 = S/10
100  PRINT "MEAN OF SCORES IS"; S1
105  REM-STATEMENTS 110 TO 140 CALCULATE DEVIATIONS
110  FOR I = 1 TO 10
120  LET D = A(I)−S1
130  PRINT "DEVIATION OF STUDENT"; I; "IS"; D
140  NEXT I
150  END
```

In the above program you will note reference to A(I), which resembles a function with its argument. What we have, however, is a list that is named A. (Any single-letter name may designate a list.) The number or variable within the parentheses is called a subscript. The subscript refers to a specific item in the list. A(I) refers to the Ith item in list A. When I = 3, for instance, A(I) would be the third item in the list, or A(3).

Statements 10 through 30 in the program read ten values into list A, and statements 50 through 100 calculate the mean of the scores and print the result. The deviations from the mean are then calculated and printed for each individual score in statements 110 through 140.

a single letter   A list name in BASIC consists of _____.

In the BASIC expression $3*A(2)$ the value of the subscript of A is _____.   2

After the program shown executes statements 10 through 30, the value of list element $A(4)$ will be _____.   57

PROBLEM 10.1 _____

Run the program in Text Frame 1 with the set of data given.

PROBLEM 10.2 _____

Now try to change the same program into a shorter and more efficient one. In other words, do exactly the same things (calculate mean and deviations), but use as few statements as possible. Hint: Try to do the program using only two FOR-NEXT loops.

2 _____

So far we have been dealing with only one set of test scores. We found that this situation could be easily handled using a list. Suppose, however, that we desired to maintain a table of scores on several tests for each of several students. BASIC provides for the handling of such tables.

Tables are similar to lists in every way, except that with tables there are two subscripts. Tables have two dimensions, length and width, whereas lists have only one dimension, length. The value of the first subscript indicates the row of the table, and the value of the second subscript indicates the column. If a table B had four rows and five columns, its individual items would be arranged as follows:

$$B(1,1)\ B(1,2)\ B(1,3)\ B(1,4)\ B(1,5)$$
$$B(2,1)\ B(2,2)\ B(2,3)\ B(2,4)\ B(2,5)$$
$$B(3,1)\ B(3,2)\ B(3,3)\ B(3,4)\ B(3,5)$$
$$B(4,1)\ B(4,2)\ B(4,3)\ B(4,4)\ B(4,5)$$

A table has two _____.   subscripts

In a table B, $B(2,3)$ is in the _____ row and the _____ column.   2d 3d

In the following table representing B find the value for $B(3,2)$ _____, for   8
$B(2,3)$ _____, for $B(4,1)$ _____.
3, 1

7	8	8	10
5	4	3	2
12	8	4	0
1	7	3	11

3 _____

A situation calling for use of a table is described in the following example. Suppose a teacher has three sets of test scores for ten students. He wants to maintain a table of these scores in order to see how each student deviated from the mean of each test or how many points each of the students has accumulated on the three tests. The program below will demonstrate the calculation of total points for each student.

```
5    REM-FIRST WE READ THE SCORES INTO TABLE B
10   FOR I = 1 TO 3
20   FOR J = 1 TO 10
30   READ B(I,J)
40   NEXT J
50   NEXT I
60   REM-SCORES ON TEST ONE
70   DATA 68,73,56,90,75,82,85,72,92,83
80   REM-SCORES ON TEST TWO
90   DATA 74,78,63,94,80,86,83,78,90,88
100  REM-SCORES ON TEST THREE
110  DATA 80,80,70,98,85,90,88,80,93,90
120  REM-NOW WE CALCULATE TOTAL FOR EACH STUDENT
130  FOR L = 1 TO 10
140  LET S = 0
150  FOR M = 1 TO 3
160  LET S = S + B (M,L)
170  NEXT M
180  PRINT "TOTAL POINTS FOR STUDENT";L;"ARE";S
190  NEXT L
200  END
```

4 _____

Study the above program carefully. Be sure you understand how the nested loops are used to read in the data and to figure the total points for each student. Refer back to Problem 7.3 if you have difficulty following the program. In order to facilitate your understanding, the first set of nested FOR–NEXT loops (statements 10 through 50) will be examined in detail.

The first time line 10 is executed, I is placed equal to one. Then (while I = 1), line 20 is executed, making J equal to 1. Line 30 is executed, and the score 68 is read into $B(1,1)$. Next, J is incremented by 1 and line 30 is executed again (causing 73 to be read into $B(1,2)$. This continues until after $J = 10$. This means that the ten scores in DATA statement 70 have been read into the first row of the three-row table B.

When this has been completed, line 50 is encountered, which causes I to be increased by 1, making it have a value of 2. Then with I equal to 2, the J loop is executed again. This causes the second row of the three-row table B to be filled with the values in DATA statement 90. After this is done, I is incremented again by 1, so that row 3 of table B will be filled with the scores of statement 110. After row 3 is filled, both loops are satisfied, and the program continues on to statement 120.

Write out what will be in column 3 when all the scores have been read into the table. _____

56
63
70

$B(1,3), B(2,3),$
$B(3,3)$

These represent the values of which elements of B? _____

PROBLEM 10.3

Run the program in Text Frame 3.

PROBLEM 10.4

Modify the program in Text Frame 3 so that it will calculate and print out the mean of each of the three sets of test scores. Hint: Make sure that the program as given above is functioning properly before attempting to add the statements to perform this new calculation.

PROBLEM 10.5

Run the same program with some additional statements that will calculate the overall mean of the 30 test scores.

5

The DIM statement

In the above discussion of lists and tables, small lists and tables were used. When more than 10 items are to be included in a list, the programmer must tell the computer how many items he will have in his list. This is done by using the DIM statement (which stands for dimension). The same kind of statement must also be used if the programmer desires to use a table larger than 10×10.

An example of the use of the DIM statement is as follows:

$$8 \text{ DIM A}(35), \text{B}(25,25)$$

This statement causes BASIC to set aside 35 storage spaces for list A and 625 (25 $\times$ 25) for table B. In some versions of BASIC, a zero subscript is permitted. In such a version, the DIM shown will result in 36 storage spaces for list A and 676 (26 times 26) for table B.

In the following example,

$$10 \text{ DIM X}(100), \text{ Y}(12,10)$$

how many storage spaces are set aside for list X? _____. For table Y? _____.

100, 120

PROBLEM 10.6

Alter the program of Problem 10.2 so that there are 15 items instead of 10. Hint: You will have to insert a DIM statement, modify the size of your loops, and furnish the other five data items.

PROBLEM 10.7

Generalize your program of Problem 10.2 to handle an arbitrary number of student test scores, up to 100.

The INPUT statement

1 _____

In Chapter 10 a program to average test scores that involved a fairly heavy use of the READ and DATA statements was presented. Further use of that program would require changes in the program itself. Through the use of the INPUT statement, however, a program that is to be used many times (especially from a time-sharing console) can often be constructed so that subsequent use of the program does not require the user to change any part of the program. With the INPUT statement, data information is furnished externally at appropriate times during the running of the program.

To illustrate the use of INPUT, we will modify one of the first simple examples given above which used READ and DATA:

```
 6  READ B,C,D
10  LET A = (B+C+D)/3
15  PRINT A
16  DATA 12,5,10
20  END
```

The READ will be replaced with INPUT and the DATA statement deleted:

```
 6  INPUT B,C,D
10  LET A = (B+C+D)/3
15  PRINT A
20  END
```

DATA

A _____ statement is not needed for an INPUT statement.

2 _____

Upon execution (at a teletype under time-sharing) the program will stop upon encountering statement 6 and print a question mark (?) at the teletype. The data numbers are to be typed following the question mark (?). The carriage return key should be hit after the last number so that the program will continue.

? 12, 5, 10

Once a sufficient amount of data has been INPUT (here three values have been called for), the program will continue with its computation.

question mark
waits

When the computer executes an INPUT statement a _____ is printed, and the computer _____ while the input data values are typed.

26

3 _____

It is a good practice to have an identifying PRINT statement immediately preceding any INPUT statement so that the user of the program can tell what data is referred to by the question mark. For instance, our example could have included the statement

5 PRINT "TYPE THREE NUMBERS TO AVERAGE";

which would have caused the following output at the teletype console:

TYPE THREE NUMBERS TO AVERAGE ?

The program user is then alerted to how much of which data to type in. By using a semicolon (or a comma) at the end of the PRINT statement, we can cause the question mark to be printed on the same line as the legend.

Write a sequence of statements that will cause the computer to print "DATA IS ?" _____

10 PRINT "DATA IS";
20 INPUT A,B,C

PROBLEM 11.1 _____

Run the preceding program examples as shown; then modify the second example so that statement 15 is followed by a GO TO . . . statement to cause the program to repeat execution for new sets of three numbers.

4 _____

The test-score averaging program in Text Frame 3 of Chapter 10 could be made more useful with INPUT statements.

```
5    REM-FIRST WE INPUT THE SCORES INTO TABLE B
6    PRINT "TYPE NO. OF TESTS (UP TO 10)";
7    INPUT T
8    PRINT "TYPE NO. OF STUDENTS (UP TO 10)";
9    INPUT P
10   FOR I = 1 TO T
15   PRINT "TYPE"; P; "SCORES FOR TEST NO."; I
20   FOR J = 1 TO P
30   INPUT B(I,J)
40   NEXT J
50   NEXT I
120  REM-NOW WE CALCULATE TOTAL FOR EACH STUDENT
130  FOR L = 1 TO P
140  LET S = 0
150  FOR M = 1 TO T
160  LET S = S + B(M,L)
170  NEXT M
```

```
180 PRINT "TOTAL POINTS FOR STUDENT"; L; "ARE"; S
190 NEXT L
200 END
```

PROBLEM 11.2 _____

Run the test-scoring example in Text Frame 4 above with a small set of sample data for, say, two tests and three students. After completing the first trial run, run the program with the numbers from the original example in Text Frame 3, Chapter 10.

PROBLEM 11.3 _____

Modify the program in Text Frame 4 above to test the values for T and P, in order to make certain that they are within the permitted range.

Defining functions (DEF)

1 _____

During the course of programming a problem, a particular formula may crop up in several places. BASIC allows the programmer to define his own functions in order to compute the values of such formulas, so that the formula needs to be written only once.

Consider the following simple program to compute certain combinations of data as percentages of the totals.

```
10 READ Y1,N1,Y2,N2,X
15 REM-MEN-YES, NO, WOMEN-YES, NO, NO RESPONSE
20 DATA 58,36,67,48,29
25 LET T1 = Y1+N1+Y2+N2
30 LET T2 = T1+X
35 PRINT "PERCENT OF NO RESPONSE", 100*X/T2
40 PRINT "PERCENT OF MEN RESP. YES", 100*Y1/(Y1+N1)
45 PRINT "PERCENT OF RESPONSE YES"
50 PRINT "—AMONG RESPONDENTS", 100*(Y1+Y2)/T1
55 PRINT "—AMONG ALL POLLED", 100*(Y1+Y2)/T2
60 END
```

2 _____

The same computational formula, percentage of total, repeats itself for different arguments. We could have defined a special function for this computation using a DEF statement:

$$5 \text{ DEF FNP(S,T)} = 100*S/T$$

Then, in place of the formulas in statements 35–55, we could make reference to this function, FNP:

```
35 PRINT "PERCENT OF NO RESPONSE", FNP(X,T2)
40 PRINT "PERCENT OF MEN RESP. YES", FNP(Y1,Y1+N1)
45 PRINT "PERCENT OF RESPONSE YES"
50 PRINT "—AMONG RESPONDENTS", FNP(Y1+Y2,T1)
55 PRINT "—AMONG ALL POLLED", FNP(Y1+Y2,T2)
```

The use of our own function has simplified the writing of the program. In the process, it also has helped us avoid programming errors.

A BASIC programmer may define his own functions by means of the _____ statement.

DEF

3 _____

Up to 26 different programmer-defined functions are permitted in a single BASIC program. These may be named FNA, FNB, FNC, etc., through FNZ.

Which of the following are proper function designations: FMA, FNB, NFC, ABC, FN2, FNZ, 12N, $B, C2, FNW? _____

FNB, FNZ, FNW

PROBLEM 12.1 _____

Run the BASIC program shown above in both versions, first without FNP and then using FNP.

PROBLEM 12.2 _____

By merely changing the DEF statement in the second program of Problem 12.1 to

$$5 \text{ DEF } FNP(S,T) = INT(100*S/T + .5)$$

you can cause the program to run computing a rounded whole percentage. Do this.

4 _____

Functions may refer to other functions in their definitions, either to BASIC special functions or other programmer-defined functions. The arguments (such as S and T in statement 5) used in the DEF statement are dummy names, and the proper argument values are substituted by the computer when a defined function is actually used. Any variables in the defining expression on the right side which are not dummy arguments on the left side will be used with their current values whenever the function is evaluated. Thus, in the program segment

```
10 DEF FNW(B) = A*B
15 LET A = 5
16 LET B = 3
20 PRINT FNW(4)
25 LET A = 2
26 LET B = 7
30 PRINT FNW(4)
```

the values 20 and 8 will be printed.
In the segment

```
10 DEF FNM(A,B) = (A+B)/2
20 DEF FNR(X,Y) = SQR(FNM(X↑2,Y↑2))
30 READ A,B,C,D,X,Y
```

```
40 DATA 1,2,3,4,5,6
50 PRINT FNR(C,D)
```

the values read in for A, B, X, and Y have no bearing on the result printed, which involves only the values of C and D. It is equivalent to the value of the expression

$$SQR((C{\uparrow}2+D{\uparrow}2)/2)$$

Could

```
10 DEF FNA(X,Y) = SQR(FNB(X,Y))
```

be a proper function-defining statement? _____   Yes, if FNB is also defined

In the statement,

$$25 \ FNJ(K,T) = S*T-K{\uparrow}2$$

which are the dummy names? _____   K, T

PROBLEM 12.3 _____

Verify the examples shown in the program segments in Text Frame 4 by running them on the computer.

5 _____

A useful function which was not discussed in Chapter 9 is the RND (*random*) function. Note that although the numbers generated by RND are not truly random, for most purposes they can be assumed to be random.

RND, when called several times in succession, will produce a sequence of numbers *randomly* chosen between 0 and 1. RND has one argument. It effects the repeatability of the *random* sequence. When this argument is zero the sequence will repeat, and when it is not zero the sequence will be different each time the program using RND is run. (Consult your BASIC reference manual.)

The _____ function causes *random* numbers to be produced by the computer.   RND

When the argument of the RND function is _____, the sequence of numbers produced will repeat. Using any _____ will cause a new repeating sequence for each run.   zero

number other than zero

PROBLEM 12.4 _____

Run the following program three times.

```
10 LET X = 0
20 LET I = 1 TO 20
```

```
30 PRINT RND(X)
40 NEXT I
50 END
```

Next, change statement 10 to

```
10 LET X = 5
```

and run the program again three times.

6 —————————————————————————————————

The RND function is useful in statistical simulation and is the heart of many computer games. It can easily be employed to generate a sequence of integers falling randomly within a chosen range. Thus, the expression

$$INT(2*RND(X)+1)$$

will produce a sequence of 1's and 2's to represent, say, a sequence of coin tosses. Similarly, for rolling dice, the expression

$$INT(6*RND(X)+1)$$

will produce a sequence representing the throws of a single die.

PROBLEM 12.5 ———————————————————————

Define a special function FND(C) for the above expression, and use it in a program to print a sequence of 100 rolls of a single die. (Leave a semicolon dangling at the end of the PRINT statement so that printing will proceed across the entire page.)

7 —————————————————————————————————

The total score on a roll of a pair of dice is not simulated by merely generating a number at random between 2 and 12. It is determined by the sum of two independent rolls of a single die. To illustrate this fact, we shall construct a program to stimulate a long sequence of rolls.

First, we define a very general function to generate randomly an integer number between given values of the arguments:

```
5 DEF FNI(M,N) = INT((N−M+1)*RND(X)+M)
```

FNI(1,6) will generate an integer number at random between 1 and 6, while FNI(2, 12) will generate an integer between 2 and 12. We dimension two lists, A and B, in which we will tally the totals for the two *methods* of simulation. Finally, we construct the program to perform a thousand *rolls* and tally the results:

```
5 DEF FNI(M,N) = INT((N−M+1)*RND(X)+M)
9 REM-DIMENSION AND CLEAR LISTS FOR TALLY
```

```
10 DIM A(12), B(12)
11 FOR J = 2 TO 12
12 LET A(J) = 0
13 LET B(J) = 0
14 NEXT J
15 FOR I = 1 TO 1000
20 LET T1 = FNI(2,12)
25 LET T2 = FNI(1,6)+FNI(1,6)
30 LET A(T1) = A(T1)+1
35 LET B(T2) = B(T2)+1
40 NEXT I
45 PRINT "TOTAL"; "METHOD A", "METHOD B"
50 FOR J = 2 TO 12
55 PRINT J,A(J), B(J)
60 NEXT J
65 END
```

PROBLEM 12.6 _____

Run the above program and examine the results. Does the correct *method B* confirm the well-known fact that seven is the most frequent total arising from the roll of a pair of dice? Insert a statement

$$6 \text{ LET } X = 1$$

and rerun the program to compare results. (Consult your BASIC reference manual if necessary.)

PROBLEM 12.7 _____

Why was not statement 25 written simply as

$$25 \text{ LET } T2 = 2*FNI(1,6)$$

instead of the way shown? If you do not know the answer to this question, rerun your program with statement 25 changed as indicated and carefully examine the results.

Matrix operations

1 _____

Because *lists* and *tables* arise so frequently in computational problems, BASIC has special *matrix*-handling capabilities. (*Matrix* is another name for *list* or *table*.) These include special matrix read and input capabilities, matrix print capability, and advanced matrix computational capabilities. Once you have mastery of the elementary BASIC features, it is worth becoming familiar with matrix operations to save unnecessary programming effort. It is important, however, to be aware of the fact that matrix capabilities in BASIC may differ considerably between versions of the language. Only very fundamental matrix capabilities common to *most* versions of BASIC will be discussed. In the programming problems you will be asked to explore possible differences in the BASIC available for your use.

matrix

read, input, print
computational

Another name for list or table is _____.

Special capabilities to be discussed involving matrices include _____, _____, _____, and _____ capabilities.

2 _____

MATREAD, MATPRINT

If a list is thought of as a matrix with only one column, then for the sake of consistency it can be viewed as being stored or displayed vertically. Thus, you can think of a four-element list L as being laid out as follows:

$$L(1)$$
$$L(2)$$
$$L(3)$$
$$L(4)$$

Then, after execution of the program sequence

```
10 DIM L(4)
20 FOR I = 1 TO 4
30 READ L(I)
40 NEXT I
50 DATA 13,6,-2,7
```

list L will hold the values

$$13$$
$$6$$
$$-2$$
$$7$$

BASIC provides a MATREAD (matrix read) statement which will considerably simplify and condense the preceding program sequence. The list L could be read in with one statement

MATREAD L

and the FOR-NEXT loop eliminated so that an equivalent program sequence would be

```
10 DIM L(4)
30 MATREAD L
50 DATA 13,6,−2,7
```

Addition of a special matrix output statement, MATPRINT, can be used to display the values of L after they are read.

```
10 DIM L(4)
30 MATREAD L
50 DATA 13,6,−2,7
60 MATPRINT L
```

Statement 60 in the program above is equivalent to the sequence
```
59 FOR I = 1 TO 4
60 PRINT L(I)
61 NEXT I
```

A *list* can be thought of as a _____. matrix with one column

PROBLEM 13.1 _____

Read in and print out the values of the four-element list L, first using FOR-NEXT loops and then using MATREAD and MATPRINT.

PROBLEM 13.2 _____

Rewrite and run the test-score problem from Text Frame 1 in Chapter 10, using a MATREAD statement. Add a MATPRINT to list the scores after they are read.

3 _____

The utility of MATREAD and MATPRINT is appreciated even more when using tables. Thus, the program sequence

```
10 DIM T(3,5)
20 FOR I = 1 TO 3
30 FOR J = 1 TO 5
40 READ T(I,J)
50 NEXT J
```

```
60 NEXT I
70 DATA 6,8,2,4,−1
80 DATA 18,22,7,−11,9
90 DATA −12,2,0,0,1
```

can be condensed to

```
10 DIM  T(3,5)
40 MATREAD  T
70 DATA 6,8,2,4,−1
80 DATA 18,22,7,−11,9
90 DATA −12,2,0,0,1
```

in which the data are read into the matrix row by row.

Addition of the statement

```
100 MATPRINT T
```

would result in the output of the values of table T printed row by row. This MAT-PRINT statement would be equivalent to the following sequence of instructions:

```
98   FOR I = 1 TO 3
99   FOR J = 1 TO 5
100 PRINT T(I,J),
101 NEXT J
102 PRINT
103 NEXT I
```

Note: The dangling comma at the end of the PRINT statement 100 will cause subsequent numbers to be printed on the same line if there is room. The empty PRINT statement 102 will cause printing to start on a new line.

In the program segment

```
10 DIM A(2,3)
20 MATREAD A
30 DATA 1,2,3,4,5,6,7,8,9,10
```

how many values will be read by statement 20? _____

PROBLEM 13.3 _____

Read in and print out the values of the 3 × 5 element table T, first using FOR-NEXT loops and then using MATREAD and MATPRINT.

PROBLEM 13.4 _____

Starting with the program in Text Frame 3 of Chapter 10, which deals with the three sets of test scores, construct a modified program which uses MATREAD to read in the scores. (Be certain you have included a proper DIM statement.)

PROBLEM 13.5 _____

Further modify the program of Problem 13.4 to include a list of the proper size to hold the total points of each student. After computing this list, print out its values using a MATPRINT statement. Confirm the results of your program by hand.

4 _____

MATINPUT

Just as there is a matrix equivalent to the READ statement in BASIC, there is a matrix equivalent to INPUT called MATINPUT. The effect of MATINPUT cannot necessarily be exactly achieved using other BASIC statements, as was the case with MATREAD. In the same way that the INPUT statement does, MATINPUT calls for values to be put in from outside the program whenever the program calls for them while it is running.

First note that the program

```
10 DIM L(4)
20 FOR I = 1 TO 4
30 INPUT L(I)
40 NEXT I
```

would call for the values of L(1) through L(4) to be put in one number at a time, say,

```
?  13
?   6
?  -2
?   7
```

The same program with MATINPUT

```
10 DIM L(4)
30 MATINPUT L
```

would behave the same way.

MATINPUT, however, normally expects numbers to be put in a row at a time, which we can only approximate with the plain INPUT statement.

Thus,

```
10 DIM T(3,5)
40 MATINPUT T
```

is exactly the equivalent of

```
10 DIM T(3,5)
20 FOR I = 1 TO 3
40 INPUT T(I,1),T(I,2),T(I,3),T(I,4),T(I,5)
60 NEXT I
```

The program above is only approximated by

```
10 DIM T(3,5)
20 FOR I = 1 TO 3
30 FOR J = 1 TO 5
40 INPUT T(I,J)
50 NEXT J
60 NEXT I
```

which takes the values in the correct order but expects them only one element at a time across each row as it moves down the rows. The MATINPUT does vary somewhat in its behavior between different versions of BASIC, but generally you should not have any difficulty if you adhere to the explanation offered here.

The program sequence

```
10 DIM T(3,5)
40 MATINPUT T
```

three

expects _____ rows of values to be input when statement 40 is executed.

five

It expects _____ values in each row.

The program sequence

```
10 DIM L(4)
30 MATINPUT L
```

four, one

expects _____ rows of values to be input with _____ values in each row when statement 30 executes.

PROBLEM 13.6 _____

Modify the program of Problem 13.2 to use MATINPUT in place of MATREAD, supplying the data externally. Test your program.

PROBLEM 13.7 _____

Use MATINPUT in place of MATREAD in the programs of Problems 13.4 and 13.5. Test them.

5 _____

Matrix computations in BASIC

Note: *The reader may wish to skip this section and go on to Chapter 14.*

Certain special mathematical operations involving entire matrices are frequently used in computations such as the solution of a system of linear equations. These operations will not be discussed in detail, but an example of their use will be given.

Suppose x, y, and z are unknowns which satisfy the equations

$$x \; - \; y \; +2z = 2$$
$$x \; +3y \; + \; z = 1$$
$$-7x \; + \; y \; +4z = 0$$

Because x, y, and z are not multiplied together and do not appear in any higher power (x^2, y^2, z^2, x^3, etc.), the above is called a system of *linear* equations. While it is easily solved by hand, it can also be solved using BASIC matrix operations in a program. This technique is also usable on a much larger system of equations, where hand calculation would be tedious.

First we read the coefficients of x, y, and z in the system of equations

$$\begin{matrix} 1 & -1 & 2 \\ 1 & 3 & 1 \\ -7 & 1 & 4 \end{matrix}$$

into a 3 × 3 matrix (*table*) A.

We read the constants on the right-hand side into a three-element 3 × 1 matrix (*list*) B:

$$\begin{matrix} 2 \\ 1 \\ 0 \end{matrix}$$

Putting the above two steps into a program, we would have for the first step

```
10 DIM A(3,3),B(3)
20 MATREAD A
21 DATA 1,-1,2
22 DATA 1,3,1
23 DATA -7,1,4
```

For the second step we add the statements

```
30 MATREAD B
31 DATA 2,1,0
```

To solve the system of equations we need to compute a 3 × 3 matrix C, called the *inverse* of A. We use a special MAT statement and special function provided in BASIC:

```
40 MAT C = INV(A)
```

We then compute a three-element *list* (3 × 1 matrix) D as the *matrix product* of C and B:

```
50 MAT D = C*B
```

The list D contains the solutions for x, y, and z, so we simply print the results:

```
60 MATPRINT D
```

Putting our program all together with an appropriate DIM statement, we have

```
10 DIM A(3,3),B(3),C(3,3),D(3)
20 MATREAD A
21 DATA 1,-1,2
```

```
22 DATA 1,3,1
23 DATA −7,1,4
30 MATREAD B
31 DATA 2,1,0
40 MAT C = INV(A)
50 MAT D = C*B
60 MATPRINT D
70 END
```

If the above program is run correctly, it will print out

$$.424242$$
$$-6.06061E-02$$
$$.757576$$

as the solution values for x, y, and z, respectively.

Assume we were going to use the system of linear equations in x and y:

$$x + 3y = 5$$
$$-2x - 4y = 11$$

What would be the elements of the coefficient matrix A? _____

What would be the elements of list B? _____

What would you change the DIM statement to in order to solve this system using the program shown? _____

How would the DATA statements appear for the elements of A?

21 _____

22 _____

23 _____

How would the DATA statement appear for the elements of B?

31 _____

$$
\begin{array}{rr}
1 & 3 \\
-2 & -4 \\
\end{array}
$$

5 11

10 DIM A(2,2), B(2),
   C(2,2), D(2)

21 DATA 1, 3
22 DATA −2, −4
23 (deleted)

31 DATA 5, 11

PROBLEM 13.8 _____

Verify that the program in Text Frame 5 will produce the answers shown, then modify the program as indicated in the questions above to solve the system

$$x + 3y = 5$$
$$-2x - 4y = 11$$

Confirm the answer given by your program by first substituting the answers into the equations to show they are correct. Then solve the system by hand, using algebraic substitution.

PROBLEM 13.9

Modify your program to solve the system

$$
\begin{aligned}
w + 3x - 2y + \quad z &= \quad 1 \\
-w + \quad x + \quad y + 3.5z &= \quad 4 \\
2w - \quad x + 7y + \quad 4z &= \quad 0 \\
5w \quad\quad + \quad y - \quad 3z &= -8
\end{aligned}
$$

for solution values of w, x, y, and z. Verify the correctness of the solutions by substituting by hand or by means of a simple program to do the substitution and check.

PROBLEM 13.10

The system

$$
\begin{aligned}
2x - \quad y + \quad z &= \quad 1 \\
3x + 2y - \quad z &= \quad 2 \\
-4x + 2y - 2z &= -2
\end{aligned}
$$

does not have a unique solution for x, y, and z. In such an instance, we say that the coefficient matrix is *singular* (it will not have an inverse). BASIC systems will differ on how they handle a *singular* matrix. Try your program out on this system to find out what your BASIC will do.

6

The extent and type of matrix operations will vary greatly from one BASIC system to another. Usually other BASIC MAT features include the matrix sum

$$
\ldots \text{MAT } E = A + C
$$

which produces a matrix (on the left) in which each element is the sum of corresponding elements in the operand matrices (on the right).

They also include *scalar* multiplication

$$
\ldots \text{MAT } C = (2.5)*A
$$

which produces a matrix (on the left) in which each element is the product of the constant (or variable) shown and the corresponding element of the matrix on the right side.

Probably the most useful statement of a noncomputational nature is the simple matrix assignment

$$
\ldots \text{MAT } A = C
$$

where the elements of the matrix A simply take on the values of the corresponding elements of the matrix C. If A and C are 3 × 5 matrices [. . . DIM A(3,5), C(3,5)], the above statement is equivalent to five statements such as

```
30  FOR I = 1 TO 3
40  FOR J = 1 TO 5
```

```
50  LET  A(I,J) = C(I,J)
60  NEXT J
70  NEXT I
```

Matrix features from one BASIC system to another
a. will almost always be alike
b. can be quite different

b.

Answer: _____

PROBLEM 13.11 _____

Consult your BASIC reference manual for a description of MAT features available.
Try out any of those features for which you can devise an appropriate test.

Other useful features: String variables, TAB function, GOSUB

1 _____

String variables

A computer is in reality a *symbol manipulator,* not merely a number machine. This is evident from the fact that we are able to use it for communicating in BASIC, which uses many symbols. Well-written programs will use a wide variety of legends and other displays of symbolic information.

BASIC includes special variables which take on strings of symbols instead of numbers as their values. These are useful in changing or manipulating the legends in PRINT statements or in conversing with the user of a program through *words* or *symbols,* as well as numbers. String-variable names always consist of a single letter followed by a dollar sign.

The statement

40 PRINT "POSITIVE ANSWER IS", X

could be written

40 PRINT A$,X

where the string variable A$ is earlier assigned the *legend* as its value, i.e.

30 LET A$ = "POSITIVE ANSWER IS"

Alternate conditions might result in giving A$ a different value, e.g.

25 LET A$ = "NEGATIVE ANSWER IS"

which would result in changing the legend printed out by

40 PRINT A$,X

Which of the following are proper string variable names? A$, S1, S2, S$, B3$, W$ _____

A$, S$, W$

What would be printed by BASIC as a result of execution of the following program sequence?

```
20 LET    E$ = "AN EYE"
30 LET    T$ = "A TOOTH"
40 LET    F$ = "FOR"
50 PRINT E$; F$; E$; "AND"; T$; F$; T$
```

AN EYE FOR AN EYE
AND A TOOTH FOR
A TOOTH

2 _____

Dollar strings may be *input* when needed. Thus, after execution of

10 INPUT A$

A$ takes on the string of characters supplied to it. It may then be copied into other string variables:

15 LET B$ = A$

or printed back out when needed:

50 PRINT "WHEN I ASKED YOU, YOU SAID" A$

The string represented may also be examined by comparison with other strings. The usefulness of this feature is illustrated in the following segment:

```
30  PRINT "DO YOU WANT AVERAGE OR MEAN";
40  INPUT A$
50  IF A$ = "AVERAGE" THEN 80
60  IF A$ = "MEAN" THEN 200
70  GO TO 30
80  . . .
    . . .
    . . .
200 . . .
```

The implementation of string variables is lacking in some versions of BASIC. The extent and type of string-variable features also vary considerably. Therefore, the BASIC reference manual for the computer facility being used should be consulted. The features as shown here are simple, useful examples of what is possible in most versions of BASIC.

Carefully trace through the following sequence:

```
10 LET X = −5
15 LET N$ = "NEGATIVE"
20 LET P$ = "POSITIVE"
30 IF X<0 THEN 60
40 LET A$ = P$
50 GO TO 70
60 LET A$ = N$
70 PRINT X, "IS", A$
```

−5 IS NEGATIVE

25 IS POSITIVE

What will be printed when statement 70 is executed? _____

What would be printed if we inserted the statement 10 LET X = 25? _____
_____

PROBLEM 14.1 _____

Starting with the sequence shown above in Text Frame 2, write a simple program which will take X as input and, using only one print statement, will identify X as being *positive, negative,* or *zero.* Change the program so that it will loop back for additional numbers to be input and tested.

PROBLEM 14.2 _____

Modify the program in Problem 14.1 so that after every three numbers are read in and tested, it will inquire of the user whether or not he wishes to continue, and then will stop or continue, based upon his YES or NO answer.

3 _____

The TAB function

The printing capabilities of BASIC were designed for simplicity and ease of use. However, occasionally the need will arise for more closely controlled spacing of printed output. The special TAB function is provided for this purpose. TAB is used only within PRINT statements. It does not create a value, but it does affect print spacing.

In the statement

$$100 \text{ PRINT A; TAB(30); B}$$

the presence of TAB(30) in the list will cause the value of B to be printed *after* the carriage is positioned 30 spaces to the right of the left-hand margin (*not* 30 positions to the right of the value of A).

As many TAB-function calls as are needed may be used in a PRINT statement, but the arguments must form a progressive sequence of positions from left to right, and they must allow room for printing the intervening numbers. Thus, the statement

$$200 \text{ PRINT TAB(10);A; TAB(35); B; TAB(60);C}$$

will result in the printing of the values for A, B, and C starting after 10, 35, and 60 positions to the right.

After execution of

$$300 \text{ PRINT TAB(20);I; TAB(40);J}$$

where will I be printed? _____

Where will J be printed? _____

Starting 20 spaces to the right
40 spaces to the right

4 _____

A variable or other expression may be used for the *argument* of TAB. This permits the affected spacing to be logically controlled by the program. The program sequence

```
100 FOR I = 1 TO 10
110 PRINT TAB(I);I
120 NEXT I
```

will result in the printing of the numbers 1 through 10 diagonally down the page. The sequence

```
200 FOR I = 1 TO 10
210 PRINT TAB (5*I);I
220 NEXT I
```

will do the same thing but will print the numbers five spaces further to the right each time.

From the sequence

```
300 LET I = 14
310 PRINT TAB (I+7);I
```

what will be printed *where?* _____
_____.

The number 14 will be printed 21 spaces to the right

PROBLEM 14.3 _____

Combine the two statement sequences 100–120 and 200–220 above into one program and run it on the computer.

5 _____

Example: Generating a report

The generation of a report is a task which is frequently programmed for a computer. Using the TAB function, you can easily program a report in BASIC.

Suppose you have the task of printing a budget report covering itemized expenditures for a reporting period and comparing these with amounts budgeted for the same period. The expenditures are to be grouped into separate categories, with a separate total to be computed and displayed for each category. A final set of totals is also to be computed and printed. The layout of the report is depicted by the following form:

	Actual		Budgeted	
	(amounts)	(totals)	(amounts)	(totals)
Category				
Item	———		———	
Item	———		———	
		———		———
Category				
Item	———		———	
Item	———		———	
		———		———

The itemized amounts and category totals actually spent are to be displayed on the left, while the budgeted amounts and totals are to be displayed on the right. The item amounts and totals are to appear in separate columns.

The following program will produce such a report for the fictitious set of data given in statements 500–503 at the end of the program.

```
100 REM-BUDGET REPORT PROGRAM
110 REM-READ VALUES FOR COLUMN ALIGNMENT
120 READ C1,C2,C3,C4
130 DATA 15,30,45,60
140 PRINT
141 PRINT TAB(25);"BUDGET REPORT"
142 PRINT
143 PRINT TAB (C1);"ACTUAL";TAB(C3);"BUDGETED"
144 PRINT
150 REM INITIALIZE TOTALS
160 LET T3 = 0
165 LET T4 = 0
170 LET T1 = 0
175 LET T2 = 0
200 REM-READ CATEGORY FOLLOWED BY ITEMS AND AMOUNTS
210 READ C$
215 IF C$ = "END" THEN 400
220 PRINT C$
225 READ I$
230 IF I$ = "END" THEN 300
240 READ A,B
250 LET T1 = T1 + A
260 LET T2 = T2 + B
270 PRINT TAB(3);I$;TAB(C1);A;TAB(C3);B
280 GO TO 225
290 REM-PRINT CATEGORY TOTALS
300 PRINT TAB(C2);T1;TAB(C4);T2
320 LET T3 = T3 + T1
340 LET T4 = T4 + T2
350 GO TO 170
390 REM-PRINT GRAND TOTALS
400 PRINT
420 LET D$ = "--------"
430 PRINT TAB(C2);D$;TAB(C4);D$
435 PRINT TAB(C1);"TOTALS";TAB(C2);T3;TAB(C4);T4
440 STOP
500 DATA"TRAVEL","GAS",25,30,"OIL",50,60,"OTHER",45.78,60.00,"END"
501 DATA"STATIONERY","STAMPS",8,10,"PAPER",15,10, "ENVELOPES"
502 DATA 4,5,"END"
503 DATA "END"
READY.
```

Examine the program carefully. Note that the TAB values are read from a single set of DATA for the variables C1, C2, C3, and C4. By merely changing that single DATA statement, the horizontal layout of the report can be changed.

Note also the use of $-string variables and data for identification of expenditure amounts in the report. The occurrence of the string DATA value "END" is used as a sentinel by the program to trigger the computation of totals and the start of a new expenditure category. A final dummy *category* "END" is used to trigger the printing of final totals and termination of the report.

From examination of the program determine where individual amounts A (actual) and B (budgeted) will be printed.

A: 15 spaces to the right
B: 45 spaces to the right

A. _____

B. _____

Where will the category totals T1 (actual) and T2 (budgeted) be printed (statement 300)?

T1: 30 spaces to the right
T2: 60 spaces to the right

T1. _____

T2. _____

PROBLEM 14.4

Run the program in Text Frame 5 with the data shown, then modify it so that all amounts will be printed five spaces further to the right.

PROBLEM 14.5

Given the following data for actual and budgeted amounts for the categories and items shown, run the budget report program in Text Frame 6 with this new data properly installed in the program.

Food: Groceries: $1,121 (actual) and $1,250 (budgeted); Dairy: 278.32 and 250.; Bakery: 132.20 and 125.

Utilities: Gas: 281.50 and 275.; Electricity: 133.80 and 140.; Water: 106.83 and 110.; Cable TV: 72.00 and 72.; Sewer: 48.00 and 48.; Garbage 36.00 and 30.

Residence: Payments: 2400.00 and 2400; Taxes 653.00 and 600.; Repairs 58.75 and 100.; Insurance: 368.50 and 350.; Lawn Care: 535.00 and 500.00.

6

Example: Plotting

The use of a variable or expression as an argument in the TAB function (as was done in the program of Problem 14.3) suggests the possibility of using TAB for the purpose of plotting or graphing. As a convenience, it is not necessary that the value of the TAB argument be exact. The whole (integer) value of the argument will be used by TAB for positioning.

Thus,

$$TAB(28.35)$$

will result in positioning of 28 spaces to the right of the margin. Likewise,

$$TAB(10*SQR(2))$$

will be equivalent to

$$TAB(14.14)$$

and result in positioning 14 spaces to the right.

Instead of *truncation* (chopping off the fraction), a *roundoff* of the tabulated amount can be accomplished by merely adding a value of five-tenths (.5).

$$TAB(SQR(3)+.5)$$

is equivalent to

$$TAB(1.732+.5)$$
$$TAB(2.232)$$

which would result in a (rounded off) two-space positioning. Similarly,

$$TAB(SQR(2)+.5)$$
$$= TAB(1.414+.5)$$
$$= TAB(1.914)$$

would result in a (rounded off) one-space positioning.

The program sequence

```
200 FOR I = 1 TO 16
210 PRINT TAB(10*SQR(I)+.5);"*"
220 NEXT I
```

will plot the square roots of the numbers 1 through 16 scaled by a factor of 10 and rounded off.

A more elaborate version of the above program would be the following sequence

```
100 PRINT TAB(14);"0.........1.........2.........3.........4"
200 FOR I = 1 TO 16
205 PRINT
206 PRINT
210 PRINT I; TAB(14); "+"; TAB(15+10*SQR(I)+.5);"*"
220 NEXT I
```

where the axis has been *translated* (shifted) 15 spaces to the right.

$$TAB(42.83)$$

would result in output being positioned _____ spaces to the right of the _____ _____.

42

margin

$$TAB(42.83+.5)$$

would result in positioning _____ spaces to the right of the margin.

43

PROBLEM 14.6 _____

Incorporate the more elaborate plotting example above into a program and run it. Modify your program to plot the cube root $(I \uparrow (1/3))$.

PROBLEM 14.7 (Optional) _____

Plot a complete sine curve by using the print statement

$$\ldots \quad \text{PRINT TAB}(20*\text{SIN}(I)+30);"*"$$

while varying I from 0 to 6.4 in steps of .2.

7 _____

Plotting with a teletypewriter time-sharing terminal can be very time consuming. A ready calculation of this time should be made before embarking on an extensive plotting effort. At ten characters per second it will take a terminal more than seven seconds to travel the full width of a 72-character line. This means that the typical plotted point (assuming a printed legend on the left) would take four seconds, and 15 points would take one minute. After making an estimate for the time for the intended plot, you can determine whether or not it would be advisable to scale it down somewhat before running it.

How long would it take a teletypewriter to plot the square roots for the whole numbers from 1 to 100? _____ _____

At 4 seconds per point, 400 seconds or nearly seven minutes

8 _____

GOSUB and RETURN statements

Frequently during the course of constructing a BASIC program of any degree of complexity, certain tasks will arise repetitively. Programming such tasks over and over again becomes a tedious matter, and the repetition detracts from a clean program organization.

The GOSUB . . . statement and its correspondent the RETURN statement allow a programmer to compartmentalize repetitive tasks and computations. The task or routine to be repeated is written only once and is referred to as a *subprogram* or *subroutine*. The section of the program corresponding to the subroutine is reached by executing a GOSUB . . . statement such as:

```
40 GOSUB 200
50 . . .
   . . .
```

The GOSUB . . . transfers program execution to the statement numbered on its right. It is similar to the effect of a GO TO . . . statement. However, the section of the program starting at (in this case) statement 200 may *return* to statement 50 by executing a RETURN statement.

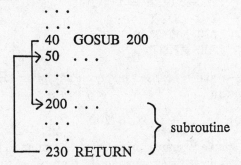

```
        . . .
        . . .
    40  GOSUB 200
    50 . . .
        . . .
        . . .
    200 . . .
        . . .              }  subroutine
    230 RETURN
```

The same subroutine may also be *called* from any other point in the program with the return to the next statement after the calling GOSUB . . . statement:

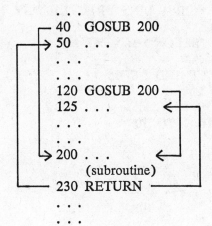

```
        . . .
    40  GOSUB 200
    50 . . .
        . . .
        . . .
    120 GOSUB 200
    125 . . .
        . . .
        . . .
    200 . . .
        (subroutine)
    230 RETURN
        . . .
        . . .
```

Complex programs may be organized with repetitive tasks programmed as _____
_____.   subroutines

A subroutine may be reached by executing a _____ statement.   GOSUB

The subroutine returns control to the next statement following the GOSUB by   RETURN
executing a _____ statement.

9 _____

A simple example of the use of a subroutine is illustrated by the following. Suppose that we want to output ten blank lines for vertical spacing. We could accomplish this simply by the program segment:

```
200 FOR I9 = 1 TO 10
210 PRINT
220 NEXT I9
```

If this is to be done more than once, this simple task could (and should) be made into a subroutine:

```
200 FOR I9 = 1 TO 10
210 PRINT
220 NEXT I9
230 RETURN
```

The above subroutine would be carried out from any point in the program by executing the single statement

. . . GOSUB 200

We can construct a simple example using this subroutine. The example will print three lines preceded, followed, and separated by ten vertical spaces.

```
10   REM GO SUB EXAMPLE
20   GOSUB 200
30   PRINT "FIRST LINE PRECEDED BY 10 SPACES"
40   GOSUB 200
50   PRINT "SECOND LINE"
60   GOSUB 200
70   PRINT "THIRD LINE"
80   GOSUB 200
90   STOP
200 FOR I9 = 1 TO 10
210 PRINT
220 NEXT I9
230 RETURN
999 END
```

PROBLEM 14.8

Run the above example as shown. Modify the subroutine so that the program will run with 15 spaces between the lines.

10

It is possible and frequently desirable to alter the effect of a subroutine by altering the value of certain of the variables it uses. Such altered variables are called *arguments* of a subroutine. We could change the vertical spacing routine to yield an arbitrary number of blank lines, utilizing an argument for the number of blank lines desired. Suppose S9 is the argument. Then the routine

```
200 FOR I9 = 1 TO S9
210 PRINT
220 NEXT I9
230 RETURN
```

would print S9 blank lines. Before calling the routine we would give the variable S9 the desired value

        30 LET S9 = 15
        40 GOSUB 200
        50 PRINT "THIS LINE PRECEDED BY 15 SPACES"

A variable whose value may be altered to change the effect of a subroutine is called an _____.

                                                      argument

PROBLEM 14.9

Modify the program of Problem 14.8 so that the subroutine uses an argument to indicate the number of vertical spaces. Let the three printed lines be preceded by 8 spaces; separated by 11 and 5 spaces, respectively; and followed by 20 spaces.

PROBLEM 14.10

Create a subroutine which will print a line of asterisks preceded and followed by a blank line. Use this subroutine in the budget report problem, Problem 14.4, to bracket the report with a line of asterisks above and below.

PROBLEM 14.11

Write a program which will plot a *bar graph*. Each bar will consist of two rows of asterisks followed by a blank line. The "length" of the bar should be an argument to a subroutine which plots the bar. Plot the data 15, 5, 38, 45, 11.

PROBLEM 14.12

Modify the bar graph subroutine so that the symbol used in printing the bar is also an argument. A bar graph may then look like this:

                    AAAAAA
                    AAAAAA

                    BBBBBBBBBB
                    BBBBBBBBBB

                    CCCC
                    CCCC

11

A subroutine may also use a GOSUB . . . statement to call another subroutine. The RETURN of the second subroutine will transfer execution back to the statement following the GOSUB in the first subroutine (*not* the statement following the GOSUB which *called* the first subroutine).

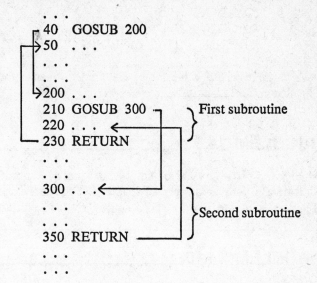

PROBLEM 14.13 _____

Find another program either from among the exercises in this book or one of your choosing which could utilize subroutines. If possible use a subroutine that uses GOSUB . . . statements to call other subroutines.

Using BASIC on a time-sharing terminal

The instructions in this appendix describe the use of a typical time-sharing terminal such as a Teletype Model 33 connected to a computer system supporting the BASIC language. *Time-sharing* is a method of using a computer to serve many terminals simultaneously in such a way that each user has the impression that his terminal is functioning as a computer devoting its time exclusively to him.

A computer will typically be connected to a time-sharing terminal by a telephone line. The terminal may be attached to the phone line directly, with contact established by dialing a number and pushing a button. Or, the terminal may connect through an ordinary telephone handset through a *box* containing a microphone and earphone to transmit a special data tone. Such a box is called an *acoustic coupler*. Once contact is established over the telephone, the handset must be firmly inserted into the coupler.

Logging on the computer

Once the terminal is connected to the computer, the computer will usually respond with an identifying message and ask the user to identify himself.

> 80/04/19   10:55.15
> UNIV. OF NEVADA TIMESHARING
> USERNUMBER:

At this point the computer expects the user to *log on* with his specially assigned identifying number and name. (The user's typed input will be shown here as underscored.)

> USERNUMBER: AB34WO5,RICHARDSON

It may also then ask for a password which for security might be typed in a blacked out area.

> PASSWORD

If the log on information is accepted, the computer is ready to respond to its special time-sharing commands and might indicate this with the output

> TERMINAL 33
> SYSTEM:

Your first command will probably be a request to use BASIC.

> SYSTEM: BASIC

The computer may then need to know whether this is a new program, an old program previously inserted, or a request for an existing program available to all users from its program *library*.

> OLD, NEW, OR LIB:

You would respond accordingly, and to start with your response would be

> OLD, NEW, OR LIB: NEW

The computer may then need to know the

PROGRAM NAME:

You devise an appropriate name and respond

PROGRAM NAME: <u>FIRST</u>

Then computer will respond with something like

READY.

(Note that some computers may respond at this point by typing a single character such as > or * to prompt *your* next response. Such a character is called a *prompt character*.)

If another program is present (an OLD program or the NEW program of a previous user already logged on your terminal) you may also need to type the command

<u>CLEAR</u>

Again the computer may respond

READY.

On most computer systems it is necessary to type a *carriage return* at the end of each line of input. Otherwise, the computer may fail to respond to your request.

Programming with BASIC

You may now enter your BASIC program, statement by statement:

10 LET A = B + C

(From here on examples of user input will not be underscored.)

Every BASIC statement which you enter must have a number. No two statements will ever have the same number, since BASIC will always replace a previously stored statement by the latest statement possessing the same number. Thus the two entries

10 LET A = B + C
10 PRINT "STATEMENT 10"

will result in the elimination of 10 LET A = B + C and the storage of 10 PRINT "STATEMENT 10".

The entry

10

—simply a statement number 10 followed by a carriage return, will result in the *deletion* of any previously stored statement numbered 10.

Under *time-sharing* BASIC keeps all statements in numeric order. Thus, you can enter

5 LET A = 1
3 LET B = 2
8 LET C = 3

and when the LIST command is given BASIC will display the statements in order:

$$3 \ LET \ B = 2$$
$$5 \ LET \ A = 1$$
$$8 \ LET \ C = 3$$

Typing mistakes are easily corrected in time-sharing. Simply follow any bad character by hitting the special erase character or keys. (See Appendix C.) The computer will delete the bad character internally.

$$10 \ LT\leftarrow ET \ A+\leftarrow = B + C$$

The above line will be stored by the computer as

$$10 \ LET \ A = B + C$$

Multiple erasures will result in the deletion of multiple preceding characters (including spaces). Thus,

$$15 \ LET \ A=B\leftarrow\leftarrow\leftarrow C=D+E$$

will be stored by the computer as

$$15 \ LET \ C=D+E$$

Some computers provide means to cancel an entire line before you hit the carriage return. After typing the special character or key for this purpose (such as ESC) the computer will respond with a carriage return and you may start over with your entry.

After typing in your program you may, if you desire, list all of your program by typing the command

LIST

and the *entire* program will be listed on the teletype. Some computers will allow you to list only a portion of the program by specifying the range of line numbers to be listed. For example

LIST 5−25

might result in a sequential listing of all line numbers existing from 5 to 25. The command

LIST 5   or   LIST,5

will result in the listing of line 5 only (if any such line) or begin listing at line 5.

When you have your entire program entered you may run it by typing the command

RUN

If there are obvious mistakes in your program, that is, if there are violations of rules of BASIC, the first result of this run will be a list of all of the errors the computer has found.† The errors will be identified by statement number and a terse explanation. For example:

$$15 \ ** \ BAD \ FORMULA \ **$$
$$120 \ ** \ FOR \ WITHOUT \ NEXT \ **$$
$$130 \ ** \ UNDEFINED \ LINE \ NUMBER \ **$$

---

† NOTE: Some BASIC systems operate *conversationally* so that errors immediately detectable in a statement are caught and mentioned when the statement is put in. However, even with a *conversational* system, RUN will be necessary to detect the remaining errors.

Examine your list and make the appropriate corrections, inserting and replacing lines as necessary. RUN the program again. If more errors are printed, continue with the correction process. Once the obvious errors are eliminated, other errors may occur while the program is running, causing it to stop after printing a message such as

220 ** RETURN BEFORE GOSUB **

These *run-time* errors along with any erroneous results are problems of your program logic. The statement number associated with a run-time error message may only be a clue. If correcting such errors becomes too involved, it may be best to spend some time going through your program *away* from the computer. In such circumstances always work with an up-to-date list of the program.

If BASIC detects no obvious errors then the computer will type the date and time and immediately execute your program.

Saving a program

To save a program for later use, type the command

SAVE

Your program will be saved by the name FIRST or whatever name you may have chosen. It can be loaded again at any time by requesting

OLD,FIRST

It can also be accessed when you next log on at the time the computer requests

OLD, NEW, OR LIB: OLD
PROGRAM NAME: FIRST

Stopping a program

Sometimes while a program is being LISTed or RUN you may wish to halt the process. A special signal is usually provided for this purpose such as hitting the S or I keys to *stop* or *interrupt* or you may simply type

STOP

if nothing is happening.

Resequencing line numbers

A good practice in BASIC programming is to use line numbers which increase in sequence by 10. This leaves room for later insertion of additional statements while maintaining the logical order of your program. Sometimes, after many insertions and corrections, the sequence gets too tight for further insertions. Many systems provide a command to resequence the program (by tens):

RESEQ

When the job of resequencing is done the computer will respond

READY.

The resequencing command will take care of all GO TO and other statements which make reference to any line number changed as a result of resequencing. *You should always LIST a resequenced program before doing any further work with it.*

Purging or deleting OLD programs

There may be limited space in your computer for the storage of old programs. Programs which you do not wish to keep should be purged or delated. Had we saved FIRST and no longer needed it we could simply command the computer to

PURGE,FIRST

and wait for it to respond

READY.

Logging off (signing off)

To sign off after your program has stopped type

BYE

The computer will print your useage statistics and terminate your telephone connection. Turn off the terminal and hang up the telephone!

Your check list

The instructions which have been given here are not specific to any particular BASIC system. They demonstrate in a general way how one usually enters and runs a BASIC program on a time-sharing terminal. There are at least five factors which in combination will affect the reader's use of his own terminal:

1. The type of terminal.
2. The type of line connection.
3. The organization supplying the computer services.
4. The computer operating system.
5. The computer type or model.

The terminal should have its own book of instructions. If there are no instructions posted beside the terminal telling you how to use the line-connecting device, then you should obtain assistance from someone who knows how to use it.

The computing center or organization supplying the computer services should provide a manual or other written instructions on how to obtain access to their computer, the telephone number or numbers, if any, user numbers and passwords, and so on.

The computing center may also have made *local* changes in the operating system and BASIC language which will result in differences with the computer manufacturer's system Operations Manual and that computer's BASIC Language Reference Manual. You should be aware of these differences if any.

Following is a check list for the reader to use in creating a set of specific instructions for operating his own time-sharing terminal for BASIC programming. You should consult the reference manuals for your computer and computer center, and consult your instructor or any other sources for the specific information needed and record it here for later reference.

Desired Action	*Specific Instructions or Command*
1. How to turn on the terminal and coupling device (if any).	_____
2. How to make contact with the computer. What is the phone number to call?	_____
3. What special action (if any) to take when the computer answer is indicated.	_____

4. How to log on:
   User Number
   Name
   Password
	_____

5. Command to call the BASIC system.	_____
6. To create NEW program (or command to call for previously stored OLD or LIBRARY program).	_____
7. Symbol or keys to ERASE a mis-typed character.	_____
8. To LIST a program.	_____
9. To STOP a program being LISTed.	_____
10. To RUN a program.	_____
11. To STOP a RUNning program.	_____
12. To CLEAR the computer before working with another program.	_____
13. To SAVE a program.	_____
14. To DELETE or PURGE an OLD program.	_____
15. To RESEQUENCE the program line numbers.	_____
16. To Log Off or BYE.	_____
17. Other Special Instructions.	_____

Using punched paper tape

Many time-sharing terminals have a paper tape punch and reader attached. These attachments should be used because of the significant amount of *on-line* time that will be saved. Tapes can also be prepared *off-line* during periods when access to time-sharing is not available. Later, with the terminal on-line to the computer under time-sharing, the tapes can be read in quickly without the delays of typing. The time on-line can then be spent to more advantage making program corrections and running the program. The time saved will permit many more users to be served during the hours that time-sharing is on, and it will lower costs if on-line time is being paid for.

Because of its importance, we will go into some detail about how to use paper tape.

All of the regular characters and key codes can be punched into the paper tape. Since you will not be connected to the computer during preparation of a tape, you may not be able to see on the paper some of the things that are typed. (Some time-sharing computers operate in the *full duplex* mode and are able to determine what will be printed at the terminal when a particular key or key combination is struck.) In any case, the effects of what you type will not be seen until the tape you prepare is read with the computer on-line.

We now give some general rules to follow in off-line tape preparation. These rules assume you are using a Teletype.

First, with the Teletype in *local* mode, make sure that the paper tape punch is turned on. Then type a series of RUBOUTs (20 to 30) to make a 2 to 3 inch leader on the tape. When the tape is read you may then position the tape ahead of your first statement. The computer will simply ignore the rubouts and will start accepting characters with the first character other than a RUBOUT that it finds on your tape. Sections of RUBOUTs may also be used between programs or multiple sets of data that are to be run using the same program. This allows time for the programmer to turn off the tape reader at proper places on his tape. After the tape is finished you may again type in a few more rubouts so that you will not tear the tape off in the middle of your last statement.

After you have punched the leader, simply proceed to type as though the console is connected to the computer. You will be able to read most of what you type on the regular Teletype paper, so there should be little difficulty. If you make a mistake typing a character, correct it in the usual manner. If an entire line needs replacing, just type another one with the same statement number. Recall that the computer always uses the last version of a statement when identical statement numbers are used.

You will have to hit both the carriage return and line feed keys while punching the paper tape. Otherwise, on the Teletype paper the lines will be typed on top of each other. During typing while connected on-line, the computer supplies the line feed when you hit a RETURN. Sometimes it is a good practice to type a RUBOUT between the RETURN and LINEFEED when punching a tape.

Now for some rules about what not to do when punching a tape.

Do not type in the prompt character that is produced at the beginning of each line by some computers when time-sharing is on. It will be printed by the computer when you read in the tape on-line.

Do not type in RUN statements. This can be done after the program is read in and you have visually verified that everything is as it should be. (If there are error messages when the tape is read into the computer, they should be taken care of before RUN is typed, since any statement causing an error message to be printed may not be retained in the version of your program that the computer has.)

Do not attempt to put the LOGIN procedures on paper tape. You should log in in the usual manner, get into the BASIC system, and then start reading in the prepared tapes. (Some systems have a TAPE command to facilitate tape reading on-line. Use it first.) And, of course, do not attempt to put the sign off procedure in the tape.

We will now lay out the steps for reading in your prepared tape.

Be certain that the machine is on-line to the computer. There is no need to read unless proper LOGIN procedures have been followed and your console is connected to the computer. Also be certain that you have threaded the tape properly. To do this, first release the tape lid on the tape reader by pushing its latch to the side. Place the beginning of the tape properly over the tape feed sprocket. Upside down or backwards tapes do not make a lot of sense to the computer. Be certain that the tiny guide holes to the left of the center in the tape engage the guide sprocket. Then close the lid over the tape and turn the reader on. It is a good idea to ask for assistance from someone with experience when you thread your first tape into the tape reader.

Let the tape reader run until your program is entirely read in. With most terminals and systems you will be able to observe progress from the listing on the Teletypewriter. NOTE: On some systems, if a bell starts ringing, turn off the tape reader immediately. The ringing bell indicates that material is being sent to the computer faster than it can be handled. If you fail to turn the tape reader off immediately, some of your program may be lost, forcing you to type parts of it over. You may turn it back on when the typing stops. On that type of system most programmers who use paper tape make it a practice to turn off the tape reader after every two or three lines to allow the computer to catch up.

After all of the program is read in, scan the listing for error messages. If you find any errors, take the necessary action and check to make sure that all of your program is there. If parts appear to be missing, type LIST and hit the RETURN key to confirm what is present. If the new listing does not contain the missing statements, then they must be typed in separately. It is a good idea to have with you the Teletype paper list of your program that was printed as you punched your tape. This will be useful in checking for missing sections and other errors.

When you are certain that the program is as you want it, type RUN and hit RETURN. If, as a result of running, some corrections are called for, make them in the manner described earlier in the Appendix. If everything appears to be satisfactory and you desire to move to another program, simply type CLEAR and hit RETURN. This clears your work space in the computer. If desired, a new tape of the modified program can be made before clearing. Simply type LIST and then turn on the tape punch. After making a new tape and clearing you are ready to turn on the tape reader again to insert another prepared program.

The precise tape procedure to fit your computer situation may vary slightly from what has been described here. From your manuals and other sources of information, prepare a checklist for your proper tape procedure.

Tape use check list and notes

Tape use check list and notes

Program case studies

This appendix includes five representative programs illustrating instructional and computational applications. Each example lists the programming background required by chapters from the text. The programs in order of presentation are:

1. Bank Balance Calculation
2. Bank Checking Account Program
3. Prime Number Generator (Elementary Version)
4. Prime Number Generator
5. Pearson Product Correlation

BANK BALANCE CALCULATION

```
00010 REM ***BANK BALANCE CALCULATION***
00020 REM  BACKGROUND: CHAPTERS 1-6.
00030 REM STARTING WITH THE INITIAL BALANCE ALL TRANSACTION AMOUNTS
00040 REM ARE ADDED TO IT (CHECKS < 0 AND DEPOSITS > 0) YIELDING
00050 REM A RUNNING TOTAL (BALANCE).  A ZERO VALUED TRANSACTION
00060 REM TERMINATES THE PROGRAM.
00070 DATA 532.48
00080 DATA -10.63,-20.21,-14.82,-129.50,-101.00,-5.95,-4.62,+56.00
00090 DATA -142.00,+410.38,-73.15,-21.00
00100 DATA 0
00110 REM READ INITIAL BALANCE.
00120 READ B
00130 PRINT "YOUR INITIAL BALANCE WAS $";B
00140 PRINT
00150 PRINT "CHECK","DEPOSIT","BALANCE"
00160 PRINT
00170 REM READ TRANSACTION
00180 READ T
00185 LET B = B + T
00190 REM LOOK FOR END.
00200 IF T = 0 THEN 300
00210 REM DEPOSIT OR CHECK?
00220 IF T > 0 THEN 270
00230 REM CHECK
00240 PRINT -T," ",B
00250 GO TO 180
00260 REM DEPOSIT
00270 PRINT " ",T,B
00280 GO TO 180
00290 REM END OF RUN
00300 PRINT
00310 PRINT "YOUR FINAL ACCOUNT BAL. IS $";B
00320 IF B >= 0 THEN 999
00330 PRINT "****O V E R D R A F T****"
00999 END
```

BANK CHECKING ACCOUNT PROGRAM

```
00010 REM ***BANK CHECKING ACCOUNT PROGRAM***
00020 REM BACKGROUND: CHAPTERS 1-10
00030 REM THIS PROGRAM SIMULATES THE HANDLING BY A BANK OF A NUMBER
00040 REM OF SEPARATE CHECKING ACCOUNTS.  EACH ACCOUNT IS
00050 REM IDENTIFIED BY A NUMBER BETWEEN ONE AND TEN.  TRANSACTIONS
00060 REM ARE ACCEPTED AT RANDOM AS A PAIR OF NUMBERS: THE ACCOUNT
00070 REM NUMBER AND THE AMOUNT OF THE TRANSACTION.  NEGATIVE AMOUNTS
00080 REM STAND FOR CHECKS AND WITHDRAWALS WHILE POSITIVE AMOUNTS
00090 REM STAND FOR DEPOSITS.
00100 REM THE ACCOUNT NUMBER IS USED BY THE PROGRAM AS A SUBSCRIPT
00110 REM TO ACCESS ELEMENTS IN A LIST "A" OF ACCOUNT BALANCES.
00120 REM A PAIR  0,0 END PROCESSING.
00150 DATA 385.63,998.71,401.22,699.00,2504.00,102.80,725.43
00155 DATA 221.33,1535.80,25.00
00160 REM  END OF CURRENT ACCOUNT BALANCES, TRANSACTIONS BELOW-
00161 DATA 1,12.35, 3,-71.40, 4,-32.51, 2,-78.95, 3,-14.18
00162 DATA 2,-21.82, 8,876.40, 9,65.80, 7,-120.00
00163 DATA 6,-45.00, 7,-120.00, 1,256.00
00169 DATA 0,0
00170 REM READ CURRENT ACCOUNT BALANCES
00175 FOR N = 1 TO 10
00180 READ A(N)
00190 NEXT N
00200 REM PROCESS TRANSACTIONS- READ ACCT. NO., AMOUNT.
00210 READ N,T
00220 IF N = 0 THEN 310
00230 IF N > 10 THEN 280
00235 IF N < 1 THEN 280
00240 A(N) = A(N) + T
00250 IF A(N) >= 0 THEN 210
00260 PRINT "**ACCOUNT**"; N; "**OVERDRAFT**"
00270 GO TO 210
00280 PRINT "**ERRONEOUS ACCOUNT NO.**";N;T
00290 GO TO 210
00300 REM END OF PROCESSING, WRITE BALANCES.
00310 PRINT
00320 PRINT "ACCT. NO.","ENDING BAL."
00330 PRINT
00340 FOR N = 1 TO 10
00350 PRINT N,A(N)
00360 NEXT N
00999 END
```

PRIME NUMBER GENERATOR
(ELEMENTARY VERSION)

```
00010 REM ***PRIME NUMBER GENERATOR (ELEMENTARY VERSION)***
00020 REM BACKGROUND: CHAPTERS 1-7.
00030 REM THIS PROGRAM GENERATES A LIST OF PRIMES UP TO THE GIVEN
00040 REM LIMIT L.   IT USES A SIMPLE SCHEME CHECKING ALL ODD NUMBERS
00050 REM N <= L FOR DIVISIBILITY BY ANY ODD NUMBER K <= SQR(N).
00060 REM THE PRIMES 2,3,5,7 ARE ALWAYS PRINTED.
00080 DATA 1000
00090 READ L
00100 PRINT "LIST OF PRIMES <=";L
00110 PRINT
00120 PRINT 2;3;5;7;
00130 FOR N = 9 TO L STEP 2
00140 FOR K = 3 TO SQR(N) STEP 2
00150 IF INT(N/K) = N/K THEN 190
00160 NEXT K
00170 REM NOT DIVISIBLE BY ANY K, SO N IS PRIME.
00180 PRINT N;
00190 NEXT N
00200 PRINT
00999 END
```

PRIME NUMBER GENERATOR

```
00010 REM    ***PRIME NUMBER GENERATOR***
00020 REM    BACKGROUND:   CHAPTERS 1-10
00030 REM    THIS MORE ADVANCED VERSION GENERATES A LIST OF PRIMES
00040 REM    UP TO THE GIVEN LIMIT L.   IT CONSTRUCTS AN INTERNAL LIST
00050 REM    OF PRIMES WHICH IT USES IN DETERMINING WHETHER OR NOT THE
00060 REM    GIVEN NUMBER  N <= L IS PRIME.
00070 REM    L = 1000 BELOW.   FOR LARGER L, THE VALUE 20 USED IN LINE
00080 REM    120 AND FOR L1 IN LINE 100 MUST BE ADJUSTED ACCORDINGLY.
00100 DATA 1000,20
00120 DIM K(20)
00130 READ L,L1
00135 LET P = 2
00140 LET K(1)=3
00150 PRINT "LIST OF PRIMES <= ";L
00155 PRINT
00160 PRINT 2;3;
00170 FOR N = 5 TO L STEP 2
00180 LET J = SQR(N)
00190 FOR M = 1 TO L1
00200 LET D = K(M)
00210 IF D > J THEN 260
00220 LET Q = N/D
00230 IF INT(Q) = Q THEN 300
00240 NEXT M
00250 REM   N IS PRIME.
00260 PRINT N;
00270 IF P > L1 THEN 300
00275 REM   SAVE PRIME IN LIST IF  P < L1
00280 LET K(P) = N
00290 LET P = P+1
00300 NEXT N
00999 END
```

PEARSON PRODUCT CORRELATION

```
00010 REM **** PEARSON PRODUCT CORRELATION ****
00020 REM BACKGROUND:   CHAPTERS 1-7.
00030 REM THIS SIMPLE EXAMPLE OF A COMPLEX CALCULATION
00040 REM DUE TO ROBERT PINNEO.
00050 REM THE PROGRAM MAY ALSO BE WRITTEN WITHOUT FOR-NEXT
00060 REM STATEMENTS REQUIRING BACKGROUND UP THRU CHAPTER 6.
00100 LET C = 0
00110 LET X1 = 0
00120 LET Y1 = 0
00130 LET X2 = 0
00140 LET Y2 = 0
00150 LET P = 0
00160 READ N
00170 REM NUMBER OF DATA PAIRS NOW READ.
00180 REM READ X,Y PAIR VALUES AND AS THEY ARE READ COMPUTE
00185 REM THE SUMS OF X'S, Y'S, THEIR SQUARES, THEIR PRODUCT.
00190 FOR C = 1 TO N
00200 READ X,Y
00210 LET X1 = X1 + X
00220 LET X2 = X2 + X↑2
00230 LET Y1 = Y1 + Y
00240 LET Y2 = Y2 + Y↑2
00250 LET P = P + X*Y
00260 NEXT C
00270 REM COMPUTE R FROM FORMULA
00280 LET R = (P - X1*X2/N)/SQR((X2 - X1↑2/N)*(Y2 - Y1↑2/N))
00290 PRINT "PEARSON PRODUCT R =   ";R
00300 DATA 10
00301 DATA 8,3
00302 DATA 2,1
00303 DATA 8,6
00304 DATA 5,3
00305 DATA 15,14
00306 DATA 11,12
00307 DATA 13,9
00308 DATA 6,4
00309 DATA 4,4
00310 DATA 6,5
999   END
```

Comparison of versions of BASIC

Feature	BASIC VERSION					
	Plaid BASIC Programming Language	Dartmouth BASIC vers. 6	Apple® II Applesoft® BASIC	CBM®-PET® BASIC	Radio Shack TRS-80® Level II BASIC	Minimum Standard (ANSI) BASIC
Variable names	letter (or) letter digit	letter (or) letter digit	letter (or) letter digit (or) letter letter	letter (or) letter digit (or) letter letter	letter (or) letter digit (or) letter letter	letter (or) letter digit
DEF Number of arguments in FN	1 or 2	No limit	1	1	No DEF statement	1
DIM Array (list/table) names	letter	letter	Same as variable	Same as variable	Same as variable	letter
Default size of List	(10)	(10)	(10)	(10)	(10)	(10)
Table	(10, 10)	(10, 10)	(10, 10)	(10, 10)	(10, 10)	(10, 10)
Subscripts start at	1	0	0	0	0	0 or OPTION BASE 1
Exponentiation operator	↑ or **	↑ or ∧	∧	↑	↑	∧
Line number range	1–9999	1–99999	0–63999	0–63999	0–65529	1–9999
MAT statements	Yes	Yes	No	No	No	No
RND form	RND (X)	RND	RND (X)	RND (X)	RND (X)	RND
String variables: Names	letter $	Same as variable followed by $	Same as variable followed by $	Same as variable followed by $	Same as variable followed by $	letter $
Maximum string size (in characters)	No limit given	4095	255	80 (but may be extended to 255)	255	18

The number of BASIC implementations and language variations is nearly innumerable. The BASIC features discussed in this book are found in most time-sharing versions that are implemented on larger computers. The micro-computer versions shown here are the most widely used at present and are typical in their deviations (e.g., the absence of MAT statements). The American National Standards Institute (ANSI) "Minimum BASIC" standard is shown for comparison. Most BASIC language implementations have their own unique extensions and idiosyncrasies. The important thing to know is that the features discussed in this book are representative and will permit you to get along in nearly any BASIC language environment. Furthermore, programs written following Plaid BASIC Programming Language will be largely transportable among many computers. For detailed information on most of the BASIC versions currently in use consult the *CONDUIT BASIC GUIDE,* Janet Frederick, Editor, published by CONDUIT, P.O. Box 388, Iowa City, Iowa 52244.

Using BASIC on a personal microcomputer

The same characteristics that make the BASIC language popular for use on time-sharing computers make it ideal for small microcomputer-based systems designed for individual use. Even the operational commands such as "RUN" and "LIST" have been carried over from time-sharing to microcomputers. Minor variations among computers do exist, however, and for the uninitiated user it is desirable to have very explicit and accurate instructions. Following are brief user instructions for getting started on each of the most popular personal computer systems in wide use today. The systems to be discussed are the APPLE II (Apple Computers, Inc.), the PET (Commodore Business Machines, Inc.), and the Radio Shack TRS-80 Microcomputer (Tandy Corporation). Key features of BASIC on these machines are compared in Appendix C. Additional information on some minor differences between BASIC as found on each computer and BASIC as presented in this Plaid textbook are discussed at the end of each section.

1

BASIC on the APPLE® Microcomputer

These instructions assume that you are using an "APPLE II PLUS" computer system. (Because there are some differences in language features and operational details among the several APPLE configurations, the reader is advised not to expect this explanation to conform exactly to each one.) It is further assumed that you are using a tape-cassette-based system for storage of programs.

The APPLE computer is ready to accept and run BASIC programs the instant it is turned on. BASIC is stored in a permanent section of the APPLE II PLUS computer memory. Any old programs, however, are lost from the memory when the power is turned off. (If you have a brand new APPLE that has not yet been used, BE CERTAIN TO READ THE INSTRUCTIONS SUPPLIED WITH THE COMPUTER before you proceed with this section!)

TURN THE COMPUTER AND THE TV MONITOR ON. After the TV warms up for a few seconds, the computer displays a copyright message:

```
* * * * * * * * * * * * * * * * * * * *
* APPLESOFT ] [ FLOATING POINT BASIC *
*              APRIL 1978              *
* * * * * * * * * * * * * * * * * * * *
COPYRIGHT 1978 APPLE COMPUTER, INC.
COPYRIGHT 1976 BY MICROSOFT
ALL RIGHTS RESERVED
```

Beneath the message is the "prompt" symbol "]" followed by the glowing cursor:

   ]□

on its screen indicating that it is ready for you to enter a program statement or a command following the] prompt symbol. (The glowing square, □ , denotes the cursor position where anything you type will next appear on the screen.)

You may now enter your BASIC program, statement by statement:

] 10 LET A = B + C □

following each line by pressing the RETURN key. Every BASIC statement should have a number. No two statements will ever have the same number, since BASIC will always replace a previously stored statement by the most recently entered statement possessing the same number. If you now enter

] 10 PRINT "STATEMENT 10"
] □

you will eliminate the statement 10 LET A = B + C and store the statement 10 PRINT "STATEMENT 10". The entry of a statement number alone

] 10
] □

will result in the DELETION of any previously stored statement by that number.

APPLE BASIC keeps all statements in numeric order. Thus, you can enter

] 6 LET A = 1
] 3 LET B = 2
] 8 LET C = 3
] □

and when the LIST command is given, APPLE BASIC will display the statements in order:

3 LET B = 2
6 LET A = 1
8 LET C = 3
] □

Typing mistakes are easily corrected on the APPLE. By pressing the cursor backspace key (left pointing arrow), you can back over and erase as many characters as you desire and then type new ones. Thus, having typed the bad statement

] 10 LET A * B + C □

before hitting the RETURN key (the cursor, □, is to the right of the C) you can backspace to the offending character

] 10 LET A □ B + C

and type the characters over (or move the cursor right with "→")

] 10 LET A = B + C □

finally hitting RETURN when positioned to the right of the correct characters.

To make a complete program from the statements you have thus far entered, add a statement to print a result:

] 20 PRINT A
] □

You then look at your complete program by typing the LIST command (followed, of course, by depressing the RETURN key):

```
] LIST

3 LET B = 2
6 LET A = 1
8 LET C = 3
10 LET A = B + C
20 PRINT A

] □
```

The APPLE will let you look at a single line (such as 10) by typing LIST 10 , or a range of lines (such as from 6 through 10) by typing LIST 6–10 , or all of the lines up to and including a line by typing LIST –10 , or all of the lines starting with a designated line by typing LIST 10– .

When you have your entire program entered you may run it by typing the command

```
] RUN □
```

followed by RETURN. The example shown (if there are no errors) would result in the following display:

```
] RUN
5

] □
```

showing the computed value of A printed by statement number 20.

If there are any mistakes in the construction of your BASIC statements, APPLE BASIC will stop as soon as it encounters such a mistake and display an appropriate error message such as

```
?SYNTAX ERROR IN 70

] □
```

The error messages produced by APPLE BASIC are expressed in the form

```
? xx ERROR IN yy
```

where "xx" is the name of the error and "yy" is the line number of the statement where the error occurred. (The error messages are explained in detail in an appendix of the APPLE reference manual. If the cause of the problem is not obvious from the reference to the offending line number, the reader should consult the Apple Reference Manual in Appendix C.)

After making the necessary corrections or modifications to your program you may RUN it again. It is probably a good idea to LIST the entire program and to examine it carefully before RUNning it again after making changes.

Stopping a running program

In order to stop a running program on the APPLE you must depress the combination of two keys simultaneously: the CONTROL key and the "C" key. (Push

"CTRL" down first and hold it down while striking the "C".) The APPLE will respond with a message such as

BREAK IN 25
] □

indicating exactly which statement was being executed by the program the instant you stopped it.

Another means of stopping the APPLE is the use of the RESET key. However, this will have the BAD effect of DESTROYING YOUR EXISTING PROGRAM, requiring you to reload it or type it over. APPLE does not provide a convenient way to stop the LISTing of a program that is too large to display at once on the screen. To see a particular segment of the program you must use the LIST xx–yy command where "xx" and "yy" represent the range of statement numbers desired.

Resequencing line numbers

APPLESOFT BASIC does not provide a means of resequencing the line numbers of an existing program. Special programs to do this task may be available, but this is not an inherent capability of the built-in system. It is good practice when writing a program to use line numbers that increase in sequence by 10, so that it will be a simple matter to make insertions.

Saving and loading an APPLE program on cassette

APPLE BASIC programs may be saved on tape cassettes and loaded into memory at any later time. The cassette recorder used with your APPLE computer is a standard type of recorder with the usual play, record, fast forward, reverse, and stop/eject controls. It also has a VOLUME CONTROL, and the SETTING OF THE VOLUME CONTROL MAY BE CRITICAL in the success of your use of the cassette program storage medium. The volume control setting should normally be in the range 4 to 6 ("medium range"). If you are SAVING a program (CSAVE) on a cassette it is a good idea to use a cleanly erased tape.

Assume the cassette recorder is properly connected to the APPLE (consult your Reference Manual) and a blank tape cassette is inserted in the recorder. Be certain the volume setting is at the recommended level (4 to 6). Also be certain that the tape is positioned past the plastic leader so that oxide coated tape is over the record/play head.

First press the RECORD and PLAY buttons on the cassette to put the recorder in the RECORD mode. Then type

] SAVE □

followed by RETURN. You must have pressed RECORD and PLAY first. The APPLE will "beep" before it starts saving your program on the cassette, and it will then "beep" when it has finished recording.

Turn the cassette player off.

It is probably a good idea to test cassette use by first loading a purchased demonstration program. This will ensure that the device is correctly connected to the computer.

Loading saved programs is accomplished through use of the LOAD command. Position the cassette tape ahead of the spot where the program was saved previously (either at the beginning or using the tape counter). Put the player in the PLAY mode. Type the command

    ] LOAD   (followed by RETURN)

The APPLE will beep when it finds the program and then beep when the loading is finished.

You can confirm the presence of your program by typing a LIST command before you attempt to RUN it.

Differences in APPLE BASIC

APPLESOFT BASIC has a number of enhancements to its language, which will not be discussed here. All of the major features of BASIC described in this book will work on the APPLE without modification. There are a few minor differences, however. The significant ones are noted in Appendix C. Other variations to note are the following:

Chapter 9:   There is no LGT (base 10 or common logarithm) function in the APPLE BASIC. To compute the common logarithm of X simply use the expression

LOG(X)/LOG(10)

Chapter 12:   The RND function covered in Section 5 should first be "seeded" by being used with a negative argument as in, say,

LET X = RND(–1)

and subsequently called with a positive argument with, say,

LET X = RND(1)

For further explanation consult your APPLE reference manual.

Chapter 14:   The maximum cursor position on the APPLE screen is 40 columns. The example programs using the TAB function should be adjusted to take this limitation into account.

References for APPLE BASIC

Applesoft II BASIC Programming Reference Manual (Cupertino, Calif.: Apple Computers, Inc., 1978).

Apple Computers has graciously granted permission for quotations from the above copyrighted manual in the preparation of this appendix.

2 ━━━━━━━━━━━━━━━━━━━━━━━━━━━━━━━━━━━━━

Using BASIC on the CBM PET® computer

The PET computer is ready to accept and run BASIC programs the instant it is turned on. BASIC is stored in a permanent section of the PET computer memory.

Any old programs, however, are lost from the memory when the power is turned off. The power switch is located on the back of the PET.

TURN THE COMPUTER ON. After the video (TV) display warms up for a few seconds, the computer will display

*** COMMODORE BASIC ***

7167 BYTES FREE

READY.
□

on its screen ready for you to enter a command or a program statement where the cursor, □ , is blinking. The 7167 tells you how much memory is available for your program. (If your machine has the smaller memory option, it will display the number 3071 instead of 7167.) If the machine happens to be ON already, there is the possibility that an old program is sitting in its memory that needs to be cleared out of the way. So, in either case, you might type the command

NEW

followed by pressing the RETURN key. The computer will respond

READY.
□

You may now enter your BASIC program, statement by statement:

10 LET A = B + C □

following each line by pressing the RETURN key. Every BASIC statement should have a number. No two statements will ever have the same number, since BASIC will always replace a previously stored statement by the most recently entered statement possessing the same number. If you now enter

10 PRINT "STATEMENT 10"
□

you will eliminate the statement 10 LET A = B + C and store the statement 10 PRINT "STATEMENT 10". The entry of a statement number alone

10
□

will result in the DELETION of any previously stored statement by that number.
    PET BASIC keeps all statements in numeric order. Thus, you can enter

6 LET A = 1
3 LET B = 2
8 LET C = 3
□

and when the LIST command is given, PET BASIC will display the statements in order:

3 LET B = 2
6 LET A = 1
8 LET C = 3

Typing mistakes are easily corrected on the PET. By pressing the DEL key, you can back over and erase as many characters as you desire and then type new ones. Thus, having typed the bad statement

    10 LET A * B + C □

before hitting the RETURN key (the cursor, □, is to the right of the C) you can backspace to the offending character

    10 LET A □

and type the characters over

    10 LET A = B + C
    □

finally hitting RETURN when the line is correct.

To make a complete program from the four statements you have thus far entered, add a statement to print a result:

    20 PRINT A
    □

You can then look at your complete program by typing the LIST command (followed, of course, by depressing the RETURN key):

    LIST

        3 LET B = 2
        6 LET A = 1
        8 LET C = 3
        10 LET A = B + C
        20 PRINT A
    READY.
        □

The PET will let you look at a single line (such as 10) by typing LIST 10, or a range of lines (such as from 6 through 10) by typing LIST 6–10, or all of the lines up to and including the line by typing LIST –10, or all of the lines starting with the designated line by typing LIST 10–.

When you have your entire program entered you may run it by taping the command

    RUN □

followed by RETURN. The example program shown (if there are no errors) would result in the following display:

    RUN
        5

    READY.
        □

showing the computed value of A printed by statement number 20.

If there are any mistakes in the construction of your BASIC statements, PET

BASIC will stop as soon as it encounters such a mistake. An error message will appear referencing the line number of the detected problem. For example

    ?SYNTAX ERROR IN 20
    READY.
    □

might be caused by mismatched parentheses or another mistake in the construction of the offending statement. Full explanation of the error messages is given in an appendix of the PET reference manual: *An Introduction to Your New PET Personal Electronic Transactor* (Revised).

After making the necessary corrections or modifications to your program you may RUN it again. It is probably a good idea to LIST the entire program and to examine it carefully before RUNning it again after making changes.

PET has a very helpful screen editor that allows you to change, insert, and delete characters right in the middle of a statement without typing the entire statement over. Use of this editor is not necessary for making corrections, and initially you should probably not attempt to use it. Simply correct offending statements by typing them over. You should consult the PET reference manual for instructions on using the editor when you feel you are ready to tackle it.

Stopping a running program

A program may be stopped while it is running by merely depressing the STOP key. When STOP is depressed, the computer will print

    BREAK IN 30
    READY.
    □

where the number indicates the statement that was being executed when the program was STOPped.

If you have stopped the program in this manner and want it to continue from the exact point where it quit, PET BASIC allows you to enter the CONT (continue) command. The continue feature is especially useful for stopping a program momentarily to permit reading of a display.

The STOP key can also be depressed during a LISTing. The CONT feature cannot be used to restart the program listing. If the last statement listed was number 230, for instance, then the command

    LIST 230–

would continue the listing from that point.

Note that the STOP key is applied externally. It is not to be confused with the execution of the STOP statement inside a program. However, when a STOP statement is executed, the same message will be displayed:

    BREAK IN 45
    READY.
    □

where the statement number will be that of a STOP statement. When an END statement is reached during program execution, PET BASIC merely stops and displays the message

READY.
□

The STOP key will not terminate a program if it is executing an INPUT statement and waiting for data to be input from the terminal. To stop a program waiting for data INPUT, merely press the RETURN key without entering any data. PET will display

READY.
□

If you do this accidentally when intending to INPUT data, simply use the CONT command to continue.

Resequencing line numbers

PET BASIC does not provide a means of resequencing the line numbers of an existing program. Special programs to do this task may be available, but this is not an inherent capability of the built-in system. It is good practice when writing a program to use line numbers that increase in sequence by 10, so that it will be a simple matter to make insertions.

Saving and loading a PET program on cassette

PET BASIC programs may be saved on tape cassettes and loaded into memory at any later time. The controls of the cassette recorder on the PET have the usual record, rewind, fast forward, play, and stop/eject controls. There is NO VOLUME CONTROL.

Insert a fresh tape cassette in the player/recorder. Rewind the tape. Assume that our first little program is still in the computer. Type the command

SAVE"FIRST"

where we have given our program the name "FIRST" to be written with it as a "label" on the tape. The PET will immediately respond

PRESS PLAY & RECORD ON TAPE #1

at which point you do exactly that. PET will then follow this line with the display

OK

WRITING FIRST

When the recording is complete, PET will respond with

READY.
□

You may immediately confirm that the cassette is recorded correctly by using the VERIFY command, which will cause the PET to read the saved program from the cassette and compare it with the BASIC program in memory which has allegedly been saved. First rewind the tape. Type the command

VERIFY   (followed by RETURN)

If there is a problem during the comparison, PET will display the message "VERIFY ERROR". If it does, it will be necessary to repeat the process just described for SAVE. It is strongly suggested that more than one copy of your program be saved on the cassette in case there is a crease or other flaw in the tape. You can merely continue saving copies (without rewinding) using different names for the copies.

Loading saved programs is accomplished through use of the LOAD command. Rewind the tape. Type the command

> LOAD"FIRST"   (followed by RETURN)

where the labeled program name (in this case "FIRST") is enclosed in quotes. The PET will immediately display

> PRESS PLAY ON TAPE #1

at which point you press the PLAY button and see PET display

> OK
> SEARCHING FOR FIRST

and shortly

> FOUND FIRST
> LOADING

When the program "FIRST" is finally loaded, PET will automatically stop the cassette and display the message

> READY.
> □

You may confirm the presence of your program by typing a LIST command before you attempt to RUN it.

It is possible to load the program by using the command LOAD without a label. In such a case, the computer will load the first program encountered on a cassette. If you use a label (in quotes, of course), PET will search the entire cassette until it finds a program by that name. NOTE, however, that while labels may be up to 16 characters in length, a short name such as "HELP" will match a longer name such as "HELPLESS" if the longer string contains the shorter one at the beginning. Take care in choosing names. Do not, for instance, use both the names "FIRST" and "FIRST1" for programs stored on the same cassette.

The RUN key on the PET may be used instead of the LOAD command to load the first program on the cassette. When the program is finally loaded, it is immediately executed without waiting for further commands.

Differences in PET BASIC

PET BASIC has a number of enhancements to its language, which will not be discussed here. All of the major features of BASIC described in this book will work on the PET without modification. There are a few minor differences, however. The significant ones are noted in the BASIC language comparison chart in Appendix D. Other points to note are the following:

Chapter 9:   There is no LGT (log base 10) function in PET BASIC. All other functions listed exist. To compute the base 10 log of X, simply use the expression

$$LOG(X)/LOG(10)$$

Chapter 12:   The RND function covered in Section 5 should first be "seeded" by being called with a negative argument as in, say,

LET X = RND(–1)

and subsequently called with a positive argument with, say,

LET X = RND(1)

For further explanation consult your PET manual.

Chapter 14:   The maximum cursor position on the smaller CBM PET computers is a nominal 40 columns. The example programs shown in Sections 3–5 using the TAB function should be adjusted to take this limitation into account.

References for PET BASIC

An Introduction to Your New PET Personal Electronic Transactor (Revised) (Santa Clara, Calif.: Commodore Business Machines, Inc., Copyright 1978).

CBM User Manual (Santa Clara, Calif.: Commodore Business Machines, Inc., Copyright 1979).
CBM and PET are trademarks of Commodore Business Machines, Inc., which has graciously granted permission for quotations from the above manuals in the preparation of this appendix.

3

Using BASIC on the TRS–80® microcomputer

These instructions assume that you are using a "LEVEL II BASIC" TRS–80 computer system. (Because many differences in language features and operational details exist between "LEVEL II" and the original "LEVEL I" version, you should note that this explanation does not apply to the smaller system.) It is further assumed that you are using a tape-cassette-based system for storage of programs.

The TRS–80 computer is ready to accept and run BASIC programs the instant it is turned on. BASIC is stored in a permanent section of the TRS–80 computer memory. Any old programs, however, are lost from the memory when the power is turned off. (If you have a brand new TRS–80 that has not yet been used, BE CERTAIN TO READ THE INSTRUCTIONS SUPPLIED WITH THE COMPUTER before you proceed with this section!)

TURN THE COMPUTER ON. After the video (TV) display warms up for a few seconds, the computer will ask

MEMORY SIZE?

You should merely respond by pressing the ENTER key. The TRS–80 will then display

RADIO SHACK LEVEL II BASIC
READY
>_

on its screen indicating that it is ready for you to enter a program statement or a command following the > prompt symbol. (The underscore symbol, __ , denotes the cursor position, where anything you type will next appear on the screen.) If the machine happens to be on already, there is the possibility that an old program is sitting in its memory that should be cleared out of the way. So, in either case, you might type the command

>NEW__

after the > prompt. Press the ENTER key after typing NEW and the computer will respond

READY
>__

You may now enter your BASIC program, statement by statement:

>10 LET A = B + C__

following each line by pressing the ENTER key. Every BASIC statement should have a number. No two statements will ever have the same number, since BASIC will always replace a previously stored statement by the most recently entered statement possessing the same number. If you now enter

>10 PRINT "STATEMENT 10"

you will eliminate the statement 10 LET A = B + C and store the statement 10 PRINT "STATEMENT 10". The entry of a statement number alone

>10
>__

will result in the DELETION of any previously stored statement by that number.
TRS–80 BASIC keeps all statements in numeric order. Thus, you can enter

>6 LET A = 1
>3 LET B = 2
>8 LET C = 3
>__

and when the LIST command is given, TRS–80 BASIC will display the statements in order:

3 LET B = 2
6 LET A = 1
8 LET C = 3
>__

Typing mistakes are easily corrected on the TRS–80. By pressing the cursor back-space key (left-pointing arrow), you can back over and erase as many characters as you desire and then type new ones. Thus, having typed the bad statement

>10 LET A * B + C__

before hitting the enter key (the cursor, __, is to the right of the C) you can back-space to the offending character

>10 LET A__

and type the characters over

>10 LET A = B + C
>__

finally hitting ENTER when the line is correct.

To make a complete program from the four statements you have thus far entered, add a statement to print a result:

>20 PRINT A
>__

You can then look at our complete program by typing the LIST command (followed, of course, by depressing the ENTER key):

>LIST
3 LET B = 2
6 LET A = 1
8 LET C = 3
10 LET A = B + C
20 PRINT A
READY
>__

The TRS–80 will let you look at a single line (such as 10) by typing LIST 10 , or a range of lines (such as from 6 through 10) by typing LIST 6–10 , or all of the lines up to and including a line by typing LIST –10 , or all of the lines starting with a designated line by typing LIST 10– .

When you have your entire program entered you may run it by typing the command

>RUN__

followed by ENTER. The example shown (if there are no errors) would result in the following display:

>RUN
 5
READY
>__

showing the computed value of A printed by statement number 20.

If there are any mistakes in the construction of your BASIC statements, TRS–80 BASIC will stop as soon as it encounters the first mistake, PLACING YOU IN ITS EDIT MODE! Get out of the EDIT MODE by simply pressing the Q key, or press the BREAK key, and then list the offending statement before making any corrections. The edit mode is a very useful feature that you will eventually want to learn, but it is not a necessary feature for creating, LISTing, or RUNning simple BASIC programs on the TRS–80. It is described in the TRS–80 LEVEL II BASIC Reference Manual and will not be discussed here.

The error messages produced by TRS–80 BASIC are expressed by a numeric code and an abbreviation. If the cause of the problem is not obvious from the reference to the offending line number, the reader should consult the TRS–80 Reference Manual, pages B/1–B/3.

After making the necessary corrections or modifications to your program you may RUN it again. It is probably a good idea to LIST the entire program and to examine it carefully before RUNning it again after making changes.

Stopping a running program

The TRS–80 has two means of stopping a program while it is running. You may depress the BREAK key to stop the program permanently, and this will result in a message such as

    BREAK AT 25
    READY
    >__

indicating exactly which statement was being executed by the program the instant you stopped it.

The other means of stopping a TRS–80 program is the use of the SHIFT and @ keys pressed simultaneously. This results in freezing the execution momentarily. Running may be resumed where it was interrupted by depressing any other key. The SHIFT @ temporary stop is particularly useful for freezing the display to permit reading if information is filling the screen too rapidly. SHIFT @ can also be used to stop a long program LIST at any point, resuming the LISTing by hitting any other key.

Resequencing line numbers

TRS–80 LEVEL II BASIC does not provide a means of resequencing the line numbers of an existing program. Special programs to do this task are available, but this is not an inherent capability of the built-in system. It is good practice when writing a program to use line numbers that increase in sequence by 10, so that it will be a simple matter to make insertions.

Saving and loading a TRS–80 program on cassette

TRS–80 BASIC programs may be saved on tape cassettes and loaded into memory at any later time. The cassette recorder provided with the TRS–80 is a standard type of recorder with the usual play, record, fast forward, reverse, and stop/eject controls. It also has a VOLUME CONTROL, and the SETTING OF THE VOLUME CONTROL MAY BE CRITICAL in the success of your use of the cassette program storage medium. The volume control setting should normally be in the range 4 to 6 ("medium range"). If you are SAVING a program (CSAVE) on a cassette it is a good idea to use a cleanly erased tape.

Assume the cassette recorder is properly connected to the TRS–80 (consult your Reference Manual) and a blank tape cassette is inserted in the recorder. Be certain the volume setting is at the recommended level (4 to 6). Also be certain that the tape is positioned past the plastic leader so that oxide coated tape is over the record/play head.

First press the RECORD and PLAY buttons on the cassette to put the recorder in the RECORD mode. Then type

    >CSAVE"FIRST"

followed by ENTER. "FIRST" is the name we have given our program to serve as its "label" on the tape. (You can choose any name to insert between the quotation marks.) The computer will respond by printing

*

flashing in the upper right hand corner of the screen, and when it has finished recording it will display

READY
>__

Turn the cassette player off.

You may immediately confirm that the cassette is recorded correctly by using the CLOAD? command, which will cause the TRS–80 to read the saved program from the cassette and compare it with the BASIC program in memory which has allegedly been saved. First rewind the tape. With the recorder in PLAY mode, type the command

>CLOAD?   (followed by ENTER)

If there is a problem during the comparison, the TRS–80 will display the message "BAD". If it does, it will be necessary to repeat the process just described for CSAVE, possibly with a slightly higher volume setting. Be certain to type the QUESTION MARK, otherwise what you have recorded will be loaded back in to replace what you have in memory. You do not want to destroy your program in memory until you have determined the recording is all right.

It is probably a good idea to test cassette use by first loading a purchased demonstration program. This will ensure that the device is correctly connected to the computer.

Loading saved programs is accomplished through use of the CLOAD command. Position the cassette tape ahead of the spot where the program was saved previously (either at the beginning or using the tape counter). Put the player in the PLAY mode. Type the command

>CLOAD"FIRST"   (followed by ENTER)

where the labeled program name (in this case "FIRST") is enclosed in quotes. The TRS–80 will immediately display

*

with the * blinking in the upper right hand corner while it is loading. When the program is loaded the computer will display

READY
>__

and you can confirm the presence of your program by typing a LIST command before you attempt to RUN it.

It is possible to load the program by using the command CLOAD without a label. In such a case, the computer will load the first program encountered on a cassette. If you use a label (in quotes, of course), the TRS–80 will search the entire cassette until it finds a program by that name. NOTE, however, that only the FIRST CHARACTER of the label name is used in this search. You can see that it would probably be a good idea to work with several tapes initially saving one program to a cassette until you get used to working with them.

Differences in TRS–80 LEVEL II BASIC

TRS–80 LEVEL II BASIC has a number of enhancements to its language, which will not be discussed here. All of the major features of BASIC described in this book will work on the TRS–80 without modification. There are a few minor differences, however. The significant ones are noted in the BASIC language comparison chart in Appendix C. Other points to be noted are the following:

Chapter 9:   There is no LGT (common or base 10 logarithm) function in TRS–80 LEVEL II BASIC. All other functions listed exist. To compute the common log of X, simply use

LOG(X)/LOG(10)

Chapter 12:   There is no DEF in the TRS–80 LEVEL II BASIC (tape cassette system).

The RND (random number) function is "seeded" by executing the RANDOM statement. An argument of 0 should then be used to provide a random number between 0 and 1. Any other positive argument, say X, will cause the generation of a random number between 0 and INT(X). For further information consult your TRS–80 manual.

Chapter 14:   The maximum cursor position on the TRS–80 Microcomputer display is 64 columns. The example programs shown in Sections 3–5 using the TAB function should be adjusted to take this limitation into account.

References for TRS–80 MICROCOMPUTER BASIC

LEVEL II BASIC Reference Manual (Ft. Worth, Texas: Radio Shack Division of Tandy Corp., Copyright 1978).

TRS–80 is a trademark of Tandy Corporation, which has granted written permission for quoting from the above copyrighted manual in the preparation of this appendix.

Examination on BASIC programming

Work the examination questions and check your answers with those given on page 90.

1. Each of the statements which follow has one or more errors. Identify them.
   ```
   110 LET A = B*−C
   120 LET D = E*SQR(F/(G+H)
   130 LET I = JK+2
   140 LET L = FNM1(N − 0)
   150 LET P5(Q+R) = S(T−1)
   160 LET U(V/2,W − 1) = U(3)
   170 LET X = ABSVAL(Y)↑ SQRT(Z)
   ```

2. In each program below what will be printed when it is RUN?
   a.
   ```
   10 READ A,B
   20 DATA 35
   30 READ C
   40 DATA 55, 45
   50 PRINT C, B, A
   60 END
   ```
   b.
   ```
   10 FOR I = 1 TO 2
   20 PRINT
   30 FOR J = 3 TO 5
   40 PRINT I;J;
   50 NEXT J
   60 NEXT I
   70 END
   ```
   c.
   ```
   10 FOR I = 1 TO 6
   20 LET A(I) = 7 − I
   30 NEXT I
   40 PRINT A(2), A(3)
   50 END
   ```
   d.
   ```
   10 FOR I = 1 to 3
   ```

   ```
   20 PRINT RND(X)*I
   30 NEXT I
   40 END
   ```

3. True or False:
   a. BASIC, which stands for Beginners All-purpose Symbolic Instruction Code, was originally developed at Dartmouth College under the direction of John G. Kemeny and Thomas E. Kurtz.
   b. Variable names may consist of one letter, one number, or a letter followed by a number.
   c. The number 123,000,000 may be written in BASIC as .123E↑9.
   d. A REM statement is used to cause the printing of explanatory legends when a program is RUN.
   e. A program whose statements are numbered in sequence by steps of *one* will be awkward to correct.
   f. The following FOR–NEXT loops are improperly nested.
   ```
   10 FOR I = 1 TO 5
   20 FOR J = 6 TO 9
   30 PRINT I, J
   40 NEXT I
   50 NEXT J
   ```
   g. The statement
   ```
   10 DEF A(3,5), B(6)
   ```
   establishes a 3 by 5 table A and a 6 element list B.

Answers to examination

1. 110 Operators not allowed side by side.
110 LET A = B* (−C)
would be correct.
120 Mismatched parentheses.
130 Either JK is an improper variable name or an operator is missing between the J and the K.
140 FNM1 is an improper defined function name.
150 P5 is an improper list name.
160 U is used as a *table* name on the left and as a *list* name on the right.
170 Proper function names on the right would be ABS and SQR.

2.
   a. 45   55   35
   b. 1 3 1 4 1 5
      2 3 2 4 2 5
   c. 5   4
   d. Unpredictable because of the random RND function.

3.
   a. True.
   b. False. One letter or a letter followed by a number.
   c. False. The power operator is not used in number representation. .123E9 or .123E+9 would be all right.
   d. False.
   e. True.
   f. True.
   g. False.

Elementary BASIC features

Major features of BASIC are listed below. Key page numbers, shown in *italic* type, refer the reader back to the text. **Elements** are followed by **Statements** in alphabetic order. Statement forms and specific but not inclusive examples are shown for the BASIC statements.

Elements

Constants, *19*   A constant is made up of digits, a decimal point (if needed), and a power of 10 scale factor (if needed).

Examples: 251   13.521   .0328E−4   38E3

Expressions, *18*   An expression is made up of variables, constants, list items, table items, operations, and functions to represent logically a mathematical formula or expression. Parentheses are used as needed.

Examples: A   A↑3/R
                     B(3)*LOG(3.14+C)   D(5)*E(I,J+2)
                     SQR(B↑2)*1.5E−4

Functions, other

INV(A), *39*   Inverse of a matrix A. Used with MAT statements.

RND(X), *31*   Random number between 0 and 1. The sequence of numbers is repeatable if X=0, otherwise different.

TAB(X), *45*   Used in a PRINT statement to position the carriage at X spaces from the left margin.

Functions, special, *20*

ABS(X)   Absolute value of X.

ATN(X)   Arc (in radians) who tangent is X.

COS(X)   Cosine of angle X, X in radians.

EXP(X) e^x (exponential function of X).

INT(X)   Integer value of X.

LGT(X)   Common logarithm of X.

LOG(X)   Natural logarithm of X.

SIN(X)   Sine of angle X, X in radians.

SQR(X)   Square root of X.

TAN(X)   Tangent of angle X, X in radians.

List items, *22*   A list item is represented by a single letter followed by a subscript value enclosed in parentheses.

Examples: B(2)   X(4)   A(I+2)

Operations, *6*   In their order of evaluation are:

↑   Exponentiation
* /   Multiplication, division
+ −   Addition, subtraction

Relations, *10*

=   Equal to
<   Less than
>   Greater than
< =   Less than or equal to
> =   Greater than or equal to
< >   Not equal to

String constants, *3*   A string constant (string) is a string of characters (possibly including blanks) enclosed in quotation marks.

Examples: "A"   "YES"   "NO"   "A.B 3C"

String variables, *43*   A string variable name is formed with a single letter followed by a dollar sign.

Examples: A$ B$ C$ T$

Table items, *23*   A table item is represented by a single letter followed by two subscript values separated by a comma and enclosed in parentheses.

Examples: Z(3,2)   B(4,1)   H(27,31)   R(I,J−1)

Variables, *5*   A variable is represented by a single letter, or by a single letter followed by a single digit.

Examples: A   C9   X1   J

Statements

DATA statement, *4*
Form:
number   **DATA**   constant,   constant,   . . .   constant
Example: 20   DATA   10,15,20,25

As a READ statement is executed, data will be extracted consecutively from the DATA statements.

DEF statement, *29*
Form:
number   **DEF**   **FN**   letter   (arguments)   =   expression
Example: 35   DEF FNA(B,C) = B*C*5

DIM (dimension) statement, *25*

Form:

number   DIM   list name (maximum subscript)
                 or
                 table name (maximum, maximum)   , . . .

Example: 8   DIM A(20),B(15,10),R(25)

This statement may be used to change the maximum size of any stated list or table. If a list does not appear in a DIM statement, its maximum subscript size is 10. If a table does not appear in a DIM statement, its maximum size is 10 by 10.

END statement, *3*

Form:

number   END

Example: 200 END

This is the last statement in a program. If END is reached by a running program, the program will terminate.

FOR statement, *16*

Form (variable stepped each time by +1):

number   FOR   variable   =   variable
                              or
                              constant   TO   variable
                              or   *or*
                              expression   constant
                                                  or
                                                  expression

Example: 15   FOR I = A+B TO 100

Form (for a different step):

number   FOR   variable   =   variable   variable   variable
                              or   *or*   *or*
                              constant   TO   constant   STEP   constant
                              or   *or*   *or*
                              expression   expression   expression

Example: 15   FOR I = A+B TO 100 STEP 2

Every FOR statement must have a corresponding NEXT statement.

GOSUB statement, *50*

Form:

number   GOSUB   statement number of start of subroutine

Example: 25   GOSUB   200

GO TO statement, *8*

Form:

number   GO TO   number

Examples: 15   GO TO 80
                     40   GOTO   60

When a GO TO statement is executed it causes the program to *jump* to the statement whose number is indicated on the right and to continue program execution from that new point.

IF statement, *9*

Form:

number   IF   relation   THEN   number

Examples: 15   IF   A < B THEN 80
                     40   IF   R*S=T−V   THEN 60

When an IF statement is executed the program *jumps* to the statement whose number is indicated on the right only if the relation holds true. Otherwise, the program continues on with the next statement in sequence below the IF. See **Elements, Relations** for the possibilities which may be tested.

INPUT statement, *26*

Form:

		variable name *or* list item *or* table item	, ...	variable name *or* list item *or* table item
number	INPUT			

Example: 20   INPUT A,B(2),D,C(15,1),E

LET statement, *3*

Form:

		variable name *or* list element *or* table element	=	expression
number	LET			

Examples: 15   LET   A(1) = B+C
              20   LET   G$ = "STRING OF CHARACTERS"

MAT statement, *38*

Form:

			=	array name *or* simple array expression
number	MAT	array name		

Examples: 15   MAT A = B
              20   MAT A = B*C
              25   MAT A = INV(B)

MATINPUT statement, *37*

Form:

number	MATINPUT	array name

Example: 15   MATINPUT A

MATPRINT statement, *34*

Form:

number	MATPRINT	array name

Examples: 10   MATPRINT A
              25   MATPRINT B;

MATREAD statement, *34*

Form:

number	MATREAD	array name

Example: 30 MATREAD A

NEXT statement, *16*

Form:

number	NEXT	variable name

Example: 25   NEXT I

There must be a NEXT statement to correspond to every FOR statement.

PRINT statement, *3*

Form:

		legend or variable name or expression	; *or* ,	. . .	legend or variable name or expression	; *or* ,
number	PRINT					

Examples: 18   PRINT "NEXT";A;B+C;D,"ALSO"
                    24   PRINT R,14,T,

If a PRINT statement ends with a comma or semicolon, the next printing done by the program will continue with the same line (if there is room); otherwise, it will start on a new line. If semicolons are used instead of commas the items listed will be printed closer together. A statement like 10 PRINT causes the output to skip a line.

READ statement, *4*

Form:

		variable name or list item or table item	,	. . .	,	variable name or list item or table item
number	READ					

Example: 40   READ   X1,B(3),Z(11,2)

This statement reads constants from the DATA statements.

REM (remark) statement, *15*

Form:

number	REM	any text for program listing

Example:

45 REM   EVERY PROGRAM SHOULD HAVE EXPLANATORY REMARKS

RETURN statement, *50*

Form:

number	RETURN

Example: 500 RETURN

Execution of a RETURN statement can only occur after execution of a GOSUB. RETURN in the *called* subroutine causes the program to branch to the statement immediately following the *calling* GOSUB.